Esports in Education

*Exploring Educational Value in Esports Clubs,
Tournaments and Live Video Productions*

By Paul William Richards

ISBN: 9781673224436

DEDICATION

To esports coaches who are helping students explore their dreams and achieve excellence in competitive video gaming.

ADDITIONAL INFORMATION

Free online course included with this book is available at:
StreamGeeks.us/esportsEDU

Esports scholarship available at:
StreamGeeks.us/esports

Free digital copy of this book is available at:
PTZOptics.com/book

Facebook Group : https://facebook.com/groups/esportsEDU

CONTENTS

ACKNOWLEDGMENTS

A big thank you to Jadd Schmeltzer from the Center for Educational Innovation, Emil Bodenstein from Alpha North Esports and Todd Conley from HighSchool.GG for the long conversations that helped structure this book. Thank you for all the introductions to folks in the esports industry who generously shared their time and expertise to help craft this book.

1 MEET THE FUTURE

The year is 2015 and the weather is beautiful in Los Angeles, California, where *"The Summit 3 by GIGABYTE,"* a DOTA2 esports tournament is being held. DOTA stands for Defense of the Ancients, which is a strategy-based video game that requires exceptional mental and physical skills to compete on a world stage. This year's event features the top six teams in the world competing against one another for a grand prize. The three best teams from China have flown in from around the world to compete with two teams from America and one from Europe. This event has been billed as one of the biggest "East Versus West" showdowns in history.

As expected, the event venue is buzzing with life. There are camera crews and the usual frenzy as everything gets set in place for the live broadcast. Meanwhile, players are taking one final look at their equipment to make sure everything is as it should be. Team leaders are going over strategies and giving final pep talks before the competition begins. At the same time, tens of thousands of spectators are waiting and an almost reverential hush spreads around the venue.

As the countdown signal starts, players sink into their custom gaming chairs and stare intently at the bright computer displays in front of them. Over the shoulder of one player, through a glass-covered window, you can spy a stately palm tree overlooking a quiet street in a suburban neighborhood. This is the home of David Parker, the co-founder of BEYOND THE SUMMIT. Parker is helping organize the studio that is live streaming the competition online.

The audience here is just as big, but instead of a huge stadium with thousands of screaming fans, viewers are spread all over the world inside everyday homes. The six five-man teams are playing what the industry considers a multiplayer online battle arena (MOBA) video game. There is a camera crew for this competition, complete with everything needed to create an immersive experience for the online audience. Parker and his team deliver viewers a similar experience to what audiences can see on the massive LED screens in stadiums. Live streams of this caliber today leverage new tools that allow viewers on Twitch and Mixer the ability to interact with the game that is being played and open interactive panels that will show player stats, inventories and other real-time developments.

Over the next eight days of the tournament, tens of thousands of spectators will log onto their computers, mobile devices, and smart TVs to follow the game in real-time. Teams will be competing for a money pool of $270,000, a sum that quite small by today's standards. Before the final day, live audiences will reach up to the one hundred thousand mark. Despite being separated by great distances, spectators can communicate online in the chat room and keep pace with a level of engagement that rivals what crowds are used to in traditional sports.

This is the world of esports. Welcome to the future!

Fast forward to the 2019 TwitchCon show in San Diego, California. I am speaking with a gentleman named Todd Conley from HighSchool.GG who is helping to design an esports curriculum for high schools around the country. Conley introduced me to a Mark "Garvey" Candella, who is the Director of Student Education and Youth Programs at Twitch. Together, we start talking about esports and the work I have done with school broadcast clubs. Garvey is working with University-level organizations to help prepare the education system to train students for careers in esports.

This is where our story begins. I tell Conley that he is invited to our upcoming "StreamGeeks Summit" in New York City, where we plan to bring together the top minds in the live streaming industry. Our team is already working with education systems across the United States, preparing students to seek careers in the video production and broadcast industry.

The broadcast industry which once consisted only of radio and television is now growing at a tremendous rate to keep up with online streaming media. This growth is fueled in part by esports. Helping students become better prepared for careers in an industry that combines video gaming, technology, and live streaming seemed to be a match made in heaven. Conley helped explain how middle and high school level students are often unsure of how their passion for esports could lead to a real-world career path other than competitive video gaming.

Conley made a few calls and realized that the StreamGeeks Summit could help bridge the worlds of existing broadcast clubs and newly forming esports organizations in education. Students interested in esports could learn about video production and students involved with their school broadcast clubs could help live stream esports tournaments. A few weeks later, we had worked out an agreement with the Center for Educational Innovation (CEI), who helped us with the outreach to school districts in the five boroughs of New York City. In less than one month, we planned to host a student-run broadcast of an esports tournament in NYC.

This is a book for any student, parent or educator interested in the intersection of esports and education. Throughout the following chapters, readers will uncover the need for a strong educational system that can help support student interest in esports. This book explores esports from a perspective of acceptance and encouragement where educators have the chance to find common ground that can help students excel in a sport, they are passionate about. Understanding how to make esports more educational requires an understanding of esports, video gaming culture, and the latest studies on sports and technology. By reviewing the history of video games in our culture and comparing academic papers on relevant subjects this book hopes to help students, parents, and educators find a positive future for competitive video gaming as a varsity-level sport. Through in-depth expert interviews and examples set by leading educational organizations you will uncover how a teenage pastime has evolved into an international phenomenon that has set a course to change the way the world views competitive sports. If the esports and education systems in place today can come together to channel the excitement and energy behind competitive video gaming, there is the opportunity to create an inclusive and productive culture that can embolden today's youth to take on the challenges our world will face in the decades to come.

It's important to note that this book includes an online course that reviews each topic in the book in greater detail on Udemy.com. This online course and the book's included glossary are available to enhance your learning. If you come across a vocabulary word that you are unfamiliar with, simply flip to the back of this book and look up the meaning of the word. If you would like to ask questions about a specific topic, you can enroll in the Udemy course and ask questions directly to the course instructor. Finally, an "EsportsEDU" Facebook group is available for students, teachers, and parents to collaborate and learn from each other at https://facebook.com/groups/esportsEDU.

2 COMMON GROUND IN ESPORTS AND EDUCATION

As you explore the intersection between esports and education, it should come as no surprise how useful common ground will be for communications. A helpful exercise to consider while reading this book is to imagine that you are the 13-year-old version of yourself growing up today. You have a group of friends who have played video games together casually since you were in grade school. Over that time, you have developed relationships and built an informal team that you are proud to be a part of. Together with your friends, you have learned your own strengths and weaknesses. Perhaps you have started to develop a reputation as the team leader or the trusted defender. Perhaps your friends consider you the compassionate one, who they seek outside of the game for real-world advice.

As the years go by, your team has gone through many battles and competitive games together. Perhaps you have met up at a local gaming center to play competitively in a group environment. Each member of your team has their own unique personality and naturally, you have learned to communicate about how to work best individually and as a team. To play best as a team, each player has learned how to make decisions about managing everyone's unique strengths and weaknesses. Although you are only 13, with your team, you are learning to solve advanced problems that require teamwork and communication. Winning feels good and collectively your team has learned how to make the most out of a loss.

All of the traditional values that represent the hard work and patience required to excel in professional sports apply to those who seek excellence in esports. From a perspective of acceptance and encouragement, parents and educators have the chance to find common ground that can help students excel in esports. This is not the first time in history the culture of the youth has changed in a relatively short period of time. Today, only 30% of students continue to play traditional sports past the age of 13, yet Pew Research reports that 90% of students between the ages of 13 and 17 play video games every day (Anderson, 2018).

Just like Rock and Roll's introduction in the 70s, the esports movement may come as a shock to parents and educators. Using American music trends as an example, you can see how culture can shift over the years.

From Rock and Roll to Punk and Grunge, there are trends that have often gone against the general status quo's idea of what is "normal." Culture can move relatively quickly, especially today as grassroots movements can spread online with groups of young people using social media.

New trends that are wholeheartedly embraced and defended by the youth are not unheard of. What history shows us time and time again, is that our society's youth and future will demand a unique identity and culture to call their own. The good news for parents, educators, and everyone involved with esports, is that this movement can be encouraged as a sport. Sports are deeply embedded in our culture and human history. Sports are in many ways responsible for helping generations of young people shape their identity. Societies from all around the world inherently understand the value of competitive sports.

In my family, baseball is held in high regard. My Grandfather, Don Richards, played at the professional level for the Boston Red Sox. While his career as a left-handed pitcher was brief, the pride for his achievements has been passed down to my children three generations later. My father took pride in teaching me how to play baseball, and I now take pride in teaching my son. Professional sports made my grandfather a hero and for that, our family will always hold a special place for baseball in our hearts.

Competitive video gaming today already holds the power to create heroes. Athletes who are admired for their determination and excellence are no different whether they are playing on a field or in a computer lab. Top esports athletes are just as important to our culture today as the NFL's Superbowl heroes. Powerful global forces may be fueling the growth of esports today, but that only makes the sport that much more spectacular. The tremendous growth in the sport is being powered by the internet, live streaming, and global economic demand all at once. The need for a strong educational support system for our youth will be of the utmost importance in the future. Modern esports games require players to manage multiple economies, respond with split-second reaction times, and co-operate with a group of players like a team of navy seals. It can be difficult to compare the complexities of competitive video gaming to any other sport in human history. We now live in a world where anyone with a high-speed internet connection has an honest chance to compete on a world stage. The democratization of competitive esports will give rise to a new future in our culture where world champions will pop up in small neighborhoods from a school district you have never heard of. It's an exciting time.

And it's time to take esports seriously.

3 A BRIEF HISTORY OF VIDEO GAMES

Video games have become integrated into the everyday lives of people all around the world. It's almost impossible to find a modern smartphone or computer today that does not ship with some preinstalled video game for users to play. While the study of video games has been active ever since the video game revolution took off in the early 1980s, most average video gamers today have never been taught how to "study" video games inner workings. To better understand the complex video games of today, it's useful to draw on the rich history of video games for perspective.

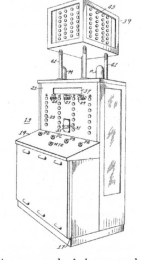

The very first computer game ever made was called the Nimatron and it was released at the 1939 World's Fair in Queens, New York. The inventor, Edward Condon, created the game based on an ancient mathematical strategy game called Nim. Nim is a game where two players, take turns removing sticks from a pile. The object of the game is to force the other player to remove the final piece. While early games like the Nimatron may seem

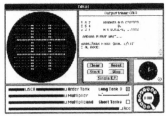

basic in comparison to today's latest multiple player online phenomenon, this is where it all started.

Another early video game was called OXO. OXO was created by A S Douglas in 1952 to simulate the popular tic-tac-toe game. In the early days of video game development, most games were created by large companies or universities. Spacewar! for example, was developed in 1962 at the Massachusetts Institute of Technology (MIT) in order to test out a new computer model called the DEC PDP-1. During the 1950s, video games were generally being created to demonstrate computing power. The games were created to research the modern limits of computer programming.

It wasn't until the 1970's that regular people started to buy video games made for the consumer market. The very first machine available for sale that was designed to play video games at home was called the Odyssey. The Odyssey gaming console was the first of its kind and the makers of the game decided to ship the device with physical items such as dice, fake money and playing cards to make customers feel more comfortable with the new idea of "video gaming." Throughout the 1970s and 1980s arcade-style video games became more popular. In 1972, a video game company called Atari created the very first successful coin-operated arcade game called Pong. Pong broke new ground for the tiny video game industry because it was so much fun to play, it caught on quickly. Like most video games at the time, Pong was based on the concept of another game. In this case, Pong was based on table tennis. The game consisted of two paddles that would hit a ball back and forth. If a player lets the ball pass them, without successfully hitting it, the other player will score a point. Pong is considered to have such a significant impact on our culture that it has a permanent place at the Smithsonian Institute in Washington D.C (Paris, 2017).

In 1980, a company called Namco release an iconic game called Pacman. Pacman was a new kind of maze game that took the world by storm. At this time most video games were being developed for a predominantly male audience. The game developers wanted to break this stereotype and create a game that would appeal to both men and women. Therefore, the game characters were made with cute colorful colors and fun-loving names such as Pinky, Blinky, Inky and Clyde. While the layout of the game is simple, it is very difficult to master. In order to master Pacman, players must think strategically about each opponent (ghost) and learn their behaviors. Pacman is considered one of the most successful video games in the world and owes much of its success to its well thought out game design.

In 1989, a company called Sega introduced its first-ever gaming console called Sega Genesis. This was followed shortly by Nintendo's first gaming console called Super NES or "SNES". This time period was great for video gamers because graphics had greatly improved, and game developers had solid platforms they could create new games for. Consoles created a market where consumers could purchase gaming systems for their homes and slowly purchase collections of their favorite games. Competition in the market forced console manufacturers to innovate. New platforms from Nintendo, Sega and eventually Sony and Microsoft started to transform the video gaming landscape. By 1994, Sony reportedly sold 102 million PlayStation console units and by 2000, Sony had sold 155 million PlayStation 2 units (Paris, 2017).

More recently the video game industry has grown at an astounding rate over the past decade. The video gaming industry has surpassed both the movie and music industry in total value. In 2019, the movie industry's estimated value was $136 billion, and the music industry was almost $20 billion. The video game industry is now about to pass $140 billion dollars, a total which has almost doubled over the past ten years. Some reports expect growth from cloud-based and mobile gaming to double the industry once again by 2025 to reach an astonishing $300 billion (Lanier, 2019). With so much growth in the industry, it's worth reviewing a few key video games and companies that have helped shape this industry with its competitive products.

Few video games have transformed the industry like League of Legends has over the past decade. The first thing to understand about League of Legends is that it's free to play and incredibly difficult to master. The game consists of two teams of five, who fight to destroy the opponent's base by using dozens of skills, teamwork, communication, memory and mental agility. The game was originally released in 2009, at a time when most video games sold for upwards of $50 to $60 per copy. League of Legends was able to attract massive audiences with their free-to-play model but also maintain high levels of engagement with a game that difficult to master. While you would think a game that is so difficult would deter players, it's League of Legends incredibly challenging aspects that have kept players coming back for years to work on their skills (Goslin, 2019).

To keep the game increasingly challenging, the game's developer Riot Games has organized seasons for the game to be played with subsequent tournaments. Throughout each season of League of Legends, Riot Games releases a series of changes through a process called patch updates. These patches keep even the top gamers on their toes by changing the game and forcing players to rethink their strategies. Each season of the game includes massive tournaments and interesting changes to the game that high school and college-level esports teams follow closely. Riot Games has effectively changed the industry's thinking about how to keep a game engaging over a long period of time by deciding to release series of game-changing patches as opposed to a sequel replacement for the game. This is a trend that almost all game developers have adapted to as the industry continues to grow and move toward a free to play model.

But how does League of Legends make money? League of Legends reportedly made $2.1 billion dollars in 2017 by selling aesthetic digital purchases to players online. It's important to note that League of Legends is not a "pay to win" game. Pay to win games have received very bad reviews in the past from gamers upset by the developer's intent to block essential game content with paid gateways. All purchases made in League of Legends are for non-essential game add-ons. These add-ons are purchased through a term known as "microtransactions." Anything that is considered essential to the game is made readily available to all players. Nonessential gaming items include character skins, hats, special items, and holiday-themed content. Some of these items are considered rare and only available for short periods of time (Goslin, 2019).

As you can imagine, with games like League of Legends it's very interesting to watch the top players execute their strategies. Because the game is so complex and ever-changing, viewers can easily save time learning by watching the top players' strategies on a live stream. The learning required to become effective at League of Legends involves serious research into the complexities of the game. So many people around the world have been actively researching how to become better at LoL it has become the most-watched video game year after year on platforms such as YouTube, Facebook, and Twitch. It's games like League of Legends that have helped grow the popular streaming service Twitch. Live-streamed video game content can be a powerful source of training that allows gamers to interact with online communities, learn how to use new vocabulary and gather the skills necessary to master a game.

On Twitch large crowds of casual gamers and fans get together to watch live video gaming and participate in an active chat room available to discuss the gameplay. Watching top League of Legends gamers explain their strategies is almost like attending an online webinar at times. Streamers on Twitch are compensated for engaging with live crowds and keeping viewers watching. Top Twitch streamers will actively answer questions from their chat rooms and give out the best advice they can in order to grow their channel and income. Viewers can learn directly from the best players in the world using Twitch through the inclusive streaming platform dedicated to video gaming. In 2019, Twitch reported that it has over 140 million monthly users. Live streaming in video games is a win-win for everyone involved. Gamers enjoy the content, streamers are able to monetize their passion, video game developers enjoy unprecedented exposure, and platforms like Twitch are able to create a lucrative business model as well.

While League of Legends transformed the multiplayer online battle arena (MOBA) genre of video games, Fortnite transformed first-person shooters (FPS) genre. Fortnite was launched in 2017 by Epic games. The game starts out by dropping 100 players onto an island where they will fight until only one winner is left. The game achieved phenomenal success in a short period of time with it's free to play model and familiar first-person shooter style of gameplay. Fortnite set a new course for the "gaming as a service" market by offering new weapons, skins, and modes to keep gamers playing. Fortnite became incredibly popular with young generations of 12 to 13-year-old gamers who are attracted to the fast-paced gaming sessions.

Fortnite benefits from the first-person shooter genre because it's familiar to a huge audience of established gamers. The almost overnight success of the game came down to a few basic elements. One the game was free and available on all major platforms, including most mobile phones. Second, the game features a strong social experience that allows gamers to play with friends they know from school or other online communities. Lastly, the game is enjoyable to watch as a spectator. Just like League of Legends, Fortnite is very popular on Twitch which in turn exposes even larger audiences of casual gamers to the game. Fortnite outgrew League of Legends in 2019, and through the process stole a significant amount of market share. In 2018, League of Legends reported that total revenue dropped from $2.1 billion a year earlier to just $1.4 billion. During this same time period, Fortnite became the world's most popular video game and grew to a record $2.4 billion in sales via the all-mighty microtransaction. Fortnite has received a lot of press throughout its meteoric rise in the esports world. Parents from all corners of the world expressed concerns about the game being too addictive. Despite some negative press about the game's addictive nature, Epic Games announced a record $15 million in prizes for the 2019 Winter Royale event. The Winter Royale event was hosted on three separate weekends each with a $5 million dollar prize. As you can imagine, with that much money at stake, the absolute best Fortnite players in the world battled for victory on an international stage with huge online audiences watching (Hitt, 2019).

4 THE STUDY OF VIDEO GAMES

Over the years, the use of video games in school systems has been adopted and documented in modern education. Research is now readily available for educators to explore the advantages that video games can bring into the classroom. While research on the positive effects of learning with video games in education is well-known, it is important to review just how quickly academic thinking has evolved over the past two decades. Today, the question on many educators' minds is not video games value for education, but it's validity as a varsity-level sport. Many wonder how video gaming culture is affecting students in school today. How will thinking change as esports become integrated into the education system?

The first-ever academic and peer-reviewed journal dedicated to computer game studies was first published in 2001, by Espen Aarseth. At the time, Aarseth was the Associate Professor in Humanistic Informatics at the University of Bergen. The journal she creatively named "Computer Game Studies" is still active today and available at gamestudies.org. In issue 1 of volume 1, Aarseth proclaims that video games are, "of greater cultural importance than, say, movies, or perhaps even sports." In 2001, online video gaming was just starting to become a reality and competitive esports were known only to small groups of informed gamers.

While the online gaming world was just beginning to develop, video gaming culture was quickly spreading beyond the niche communities of the 1980s and 90s. Early online video games such as "Ultima Online" and "Quake Arena" were just starting to give developers a glimpse at the online worlds they would be able to create in the future. Aarseth explains online gaming as "the greatest innovation in audience structure since the invention of the choir, thousands of years ago." At a time when few academic papers had been published on video games, Aarseth writes, "we have a billion-dollar industry with almost no basic research." Aarseth's first issue in *Computer Game Studies* calls for "scholars and academics to take computer games seriously, as a cultural field whose value of hard to overestimate."

Almost ten years later, in 2010, José P. Zagal published a book called *Ludoliteracy*. Ludoliteracy is a book written to help define, understand and support "Game Education." Zagal's book is a must-read for any educator interested in helping students learn what it truly means to understand and study video games. James Paul Gee, who is an expert on the subject and a Professor of Literacy Studies at Arizona State, calls the book, "the first truly modern book in Game Studies, fully aware that Game Studies is a central 21st Century liberal art." In this book, Zagal explains that there are essentially three types of video game research happening today. These areas of video game research include social studies (studying the effects of games on people), humanities (studying the meaning and context of games) and industry/engineering (creating new technologies used in games, design, and development). Ludoliteracy helped define essential questions about how students can understand and analyze video games in a meaningful way. Zagal's research suggests that online blogging can be an exercise used to help gamers reflect on their experiences.

One interesting study concluded, "Students found that by reflecting on their experiences playing games, they began to understand how the design elements helped shape that experience. Most importantly, they stepped back from their traditional role as 'gamers' or 'fans' and engaged in reasoning critically and analytically about the games they were studying." Zagal suggested that students use a website called GameLog, which was developed to help students, "leverage their game playing experiences in order to establish links between their experiences and the abstract concepts, language, and vocabulary of game studies in general." A core theme that will be discussed in this book is strategies to help create common ground for students, parents, and educators on the subject of video game experiences (Zagal, 2010).

This type of reflection and understanding of game theory will be crucial for students to master esports and develop real-world skills from playing video games. Zagal was arguably far ahead of his time with his book, as he outlines concepts to help students and teachers contribute to the academic study of video games. In a world that can look like a moving target for educators, Zagal is able to encourage tried and true methods for furthering our understanding of video game technology. Later on in this book, we will discuss, strategies to help students get the most educational value out of the video games they are playing.

Zagal's work was influenced by a book called *What Video Games Have to Teach Us About Learning and Literacy*, published seven years prior in 2003 by James Paul Gee. In this book, Gee helps readers understand what it means to be "video game literate." The thesis here is that literacy has expanded beyond just "reading a book" and a new understanding of how to "read" a video game is now needed for the study of video games. A basic understanding goes something like this. To be literate in video games, one must have the ability to play video games. One must also have the ability to understand the meanings with respect to the game. Finally, one must have the ability to make a game. From an educational perspective, it's important to keep these foundational concepts in mind at a high level when discussing esports strategy and video game culture.

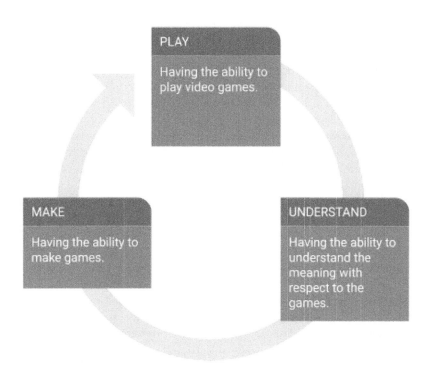

Perhaps the most important thing for esports today is having the ability to understand meanings with respect to the game students are playing. As games in esports continue to evolve and change, core understandings of the foundational game types from which these games have been built upon are crucial to the educational process. A simple understanding of the history of games should not be lost on players who may only focus on winning the latest game. Huge prizes and scholarships can easily blind players from an important educational perspective which involves the understanding of the current place video games are in history.

Today in 2020, nearly all levels of the K-12 and higher education schooling systems have access to educational video games that can be integrated into the curriculum. Many of these video games have been designed to make the student learning experience more fun and engaging. A neuroscientist from Bristol University by the name of Mr. Howard-Jones is a major supporter of video games in education, and he has the science to back him up. Howard says "computer games are very, very engaging. And just as nuclear fission can be used to make bombs or generate electricity, games also have a light side and a dark side." Howard's science refers to the studied effects of video gaming on the brain's reward system which produces dopamine, a chemical that can enhance connections made between neurons. This process Howard describes as "the basis for all learning."

Studies show that the introduction of chance in the learning process has the power to increase dopamine production triggered by the human reward system. Howard's studies have proven that students will actually learn more when they are offered the chance of a reward versus a guaranteed reward (Guttenplan, 2012). Howard's analogy about the light side and dark side is something educators may already understand too well. A core philosophy supporting the adoption of esports in education systems is to help promote the positive side of video games, while at the same time preparing students for the negative aspects that occur without proper teacher and parental guidance.

In 2009, MIT published one of the top academic papers on the subject of "Educational Games and Learning Through Play" in a paper aptly named *The Educational Arcade*. This 55-page paper is considered one of the best resources for educators who want to learn more about video games' educational use cases in the classroom. The paper's authors Eric Klopfer, Scot Osterweil, and Katie Salen help define important aspects that are key to understanding how video games can be used in education. While this paper was published over 10 years ago, the foundation they laid for the adoption of "learning games" in the educational system has been influential across the globe. The paper outlines the many barriers that have slowed progress with the adoption of learning games in education over the years. Some of these barriers have included Curriculum Requirements, Logistics, Support for Teachers, Assessment, Evidence, and Social/Cultural Structures (MIT, 2019).

Today, it seems that many of the barriers MIT's *Educational Arcade* described have been overcome with the power of time and progress. From 2018 to 2019, the High School Esports League, or HSEL, has reported the number of schools with esports programs has grown from 200 to more than 1,200.

With that kind of growth, it won't take long for every school in the country to have an esports program. As schools create frameworks to position video games as educational tools, school systems can set the stage for varsity esports programs. This paradigm shift will allow esports programs to be supported just like traditional sports such as baseball, football, hockey, tennis, and soccer.

The North American Scholastic Esports Federation, or NASEF, now offers high school level STEM curriculums that integrate esports into English classes. The curriculum seeks out, "explicit connections with esports" and builds them into an English curriculum that today's technology-savvy students enjoy engaging with. This integrated set of courses has been designed for Grades 9-12 and can be used to replace traditional high school English. The courses comply with content standards from the Next Generation Science Standards, English-Language Arts, International Society of Technology in Education, and Social-Emotional Learning (NASEF, 2019). As STEM schools push for innovation in esports, public and private schools will soon follow.

Esports is now recognized globally as a sport that can help players develop life-long skills that come from competitive team activities. While not all school districts have yet sanctioned gaming as an official sport (as of early 2020), organizations like the High School Esports League (HSEL), the High School Starleague (HSL), and the Youth Esports of America (YEA) continue to lobby with school districts to bring esports up to the current standards of sports in school athletics. Educational systems at the high school level are actively adding esports programs as school clubs, with the help of faculty member sponsors. Just like established robotics clubs, esports clubs can form teams to compete in local, state, and national competitions.

Students' passion to play competitively requires the same teamwork and dedication at the heart and soul of all sports. But esports clubs do not receive the same funding or status as varsity level sports. Clubs lack the dedicated coaches and resources needed to build teams that can compete on a national level. This is why esports clubs will eventually become school-sponsored athletic teams in the near future. Starting an esports club is a great start for any group of students who want to forge a path toward a varsity-level program.

One reason esports has taken so long to become recognized as a school sport has to do with the study of sports itself. Sports science is a discipline that many professionals in athletics study to become sports coaches, therapists, administrators, and trainers. Sports science courses are only now becoming more aware of how important the study of esports has and will become in society. Adults from all walks of life are starting to realize that competitive video gaming is a spectator sport just like college football. When educators have an open mind about the feeling spectators have watching competitive video gaming, they can realize how similar the core emotions are to the sports that have been so popular throughout history.

In 2017, three Temple University professors from Philadelphia wrote an academic paper called, "Esports Management: Embracing Esports education and research opportunities." The paper attempts to prove that esports should be considered a "real sport" and notes that, "despite growth and acceptance by consumers and practitioners, academics [still] debate esports position within the domain of sports management." The authors of this paper highlight five points that have pushed forward thinking on the subject.

1. Esport's organized video game competitions, is increasingly recognized as a sport.
2. Esport's structure, organization, and institutionalization qualify the activity as a sport.
3. Esports represent a novel area for sport management research, education, and practice.
4. Expertise from sport management can inform emerging dilemmas facing esports.
5. Organized esports events and competitions should remain within sport management (Funk, 2017).

As Gehrig Rosen of the Palomar College's Independent Newspaper puts it, "Anything that has a strong competitive format, requires a specific set of skills, great hand-eye coordination, and training, is a sport" (Gehrig, 2017). Change takes time, especially when it comes to the education system. In this book, you will be encouraged to explore the history and culture of esports to gather a better understanding of the landscape. While the future of competitive video gaming looks bright, there are many legitimate reasons for concern from an educational perspective. Howard-Jones from Bristol University put it best when he said that video games have both a light and dark side. The best way to address concerns about esports and video games is to help shepherd students toward the light side. And yes, a Star Wars reference will be well received in most gaming circles

5 GETTING THE MOST EDUCATIONAL VALUE OUT OF VIDEO GAMES

With new games coming out every month, you may think it could be a near-impossible task for parents and coaches to keep up with the latest video games. Should parents be worried about any potential harmful influences video games can have on their children? How will esports coaches discourage video games with mature and even crude content? This is a question a lot of parents and school administrators ask and their worries are justified.

Given that many games involve graphic scenes of violence and mature content that can include sexual themes, gambling, and drug use, it's no wonder parents worry. These concerns are often amplified when young people sit for hours playing games that can easily be downloaded from the internet. Luckily, a few concerned individuals and institutions have raised legitimate questions about the physical, mental, and emotional health risks posed by video games. The problem is made more difficult by the fact that most adults are unfamiliar with video gaming culture. Parents of "Millennials" also known as "Generation Y" often voice opinions about being unequipped to decide which video games are helpful or harmful to young people.

There is no straightforward answer to the question "Are video games good or bad?" This is because a lot depends on the game in question. Results can also vary depending on the individual who is playing and the way they interact with the game. However, there are ways for adults and educators to encourage productive gameplay and best practices for selecting appropriate games by age and maturity.

The Trouble with Video Games

Almost everyone has heard of the negative side effects of playing too many video games. There are physical, psychological, and social difficulties that young people who spend too much time playing video games are likely to face. These problems are real and if not properly addressed, they can generate long-term health issues. Against the backdrop of the World Health Organization's (WHO) declaration of gaming addiction as a mental health disorder, here are some of the most important dangers posed by video games.

Disconnection From Reality

Addicted gamers manifest a significant inability to stay "in the moment" because their minds constantly wander to the game. Additionally, gaming can become an escape from reality. Video games can become a safe-haven where the gamer retreats to escape the chaos of life. In some cases, gamers can lose interest in all other non-gaming activities (Holstein, 2019).

Social Isolation
Regardless of how much a video game tries to mimic real life, people still need to physically interact with others to lead a healthy life. Young people may naturally find it hard to make friends, but video games can compound the problem by denying many of today's youth the chance to outgrow their social awkwardness. The impact of this can be seen in Hong Kong's problem of "Herbivore Men." A new article from the South China Morning Post reports that "In a city already known for its low sex drive, there is a new generation of men who are uninterested in romance and relationships… technology is [reportedly] distracting them." Dr Paul Wong Wai-Chang from University of Hong Kong goes on to say that, "These herbivore men don't connect with others, they don't establish their own families or have children and don't really contribute anything meaningful to society, either tangibly or intangibly" ("Hong Kong's libido takes another hit, from herbivores and hermits," 2018).

Physical Health Issues
Lack of exercise is bad for people of any age, but especially for the growing bodies of children and teenagers. The consequences of inadequate exercise include shrinking muscle mass and increased risk of obesity, heart disease, depression, and shorter life expectancy. This is a problem that is being taken seriously in professional esports as the importance of a healthy mind and bodywork hand in hand. New studies do report that sitting all day is just a bad for human health as smoking ("Is Sitting Worse Than Smoking? – Alternet.org," n.d.).

Brain Damage
Overexposure to computer screens can affect the brain negatively. This is true for TV, computer, or smartphone screens. In some extreme cases, brain damage effects can include seizures, insomnia, and reduced working memory. There is also a higher risk of developing brain diseases, such as schizophrenia, PTSD, and Alzheimer's. Regulated screen times are critical for young people whose brains are still developing.

Addiction, Aggression, and Attention-Deficit
Video games activate the same centers in the brain that illicit drugs do. Therefore, video games can become addictive. Additionally, many gamers experience increased levels of brain activity that are associated with

aggression. Finally, even if video games improve attention, they usually do so in the short-term. Studies show video games can eventually hurt gamers' long-term attention span (Webber, 2018).

Lack of Sleep

Many students who play video games into the night suffer from a lack of sleep. Because video games are so accessible and there's always a friend available to play online, many gamers tend to play for long periods of time. Allowing students to express their interest in video gaming in class, in a group setting, or other school-related activities can make their video gaming habits healthier. Helping to bring esports into education can be a potential fix to the problem. Just look at the professional esports athletes that are role models in this area. Just like any professional athlete a healthy mind and body are considered essential for top performers. A holistic view of achieving excellence in esports requires a healthy diet, normal sleep patterns, and an emphasis on education. Educators can help students understand how a healthy lifestyle can help them achieve their own goals in relation to competitive video gaming.

ESRB Rating System and How To Identify The Best Games

The ESRB (Entertainment Software Rating Board) has developed a rating system that parents and other adults can employ to judge the appropriateness of various games for children and young people of different ages. These ratings can be found printed on physical video game boxes and are also displayed on the official video game websites ("Ratings Guide," n.d.).

The rating uses the following symbols:

·   **eC (Early Childhood)**: Equivalent to Soft G and considered safe for young children.

·   **E (Everyone)**: Suitable for all ages and equivalent to hard G and soft PG.

·   **E10+ (Everyone 10+)**: Appropriate for ages 10 & older, and equivalent to hard PG.

·   **T (Teen)**: The game is acceptable for ages 13 and older. This is the equivalent of PG-13.

· **M (Mature)**: Reserved for ages 17 and older. It is equivalent to R.

· **AO (Adults Only)**: Suitable for persons 18+ and equivalent to NC-17.

· **RP (Rating Pending)**: This means the game has not been rated, which is equivalent to NR.

Other than the ESRB system, how can you look for educational value in video games? Asking the following questions can help guide the answers to this question (Editors, 2018).

· **Usable Skills**: Does the game teach life skills, such as negotiating, analytical thinking, and teamwork? Is the objective of the game related to something that happens in real life?

· **Economics**: Do players use resources, such as money, time, relationships, and land? Do their choices have an impact on the outcome of the game?

· **Thoughtfulness**: Does the game incorporate a repetitive mode that requires only basic memorization or do players have to apply their minds to solve problems?

· **Tasking**: What is the difficulty level of the game? How challenging is the game? Are their puzzles or activities that require problem-solving?

· **Socializing**: Games that require team play, cooperation, personal responsibility, as well as, shared objectives, can teach skills that can be transferred into real life.

· **Creativity**: Does the game spark young peoples' creativity?

Video Games: A Little More Than Entertainment

Most modern technology is ultimately neither good nor bad. What makes technology useful or unsafe is the way in which it is used. The potential for abuse is real, but the potential for positive use is as well. So many good uses for video games are being discovered that the importance of proper education and mentorship is imperative. Some of the constructive uses of video games are highly innovative. There are good reasons for high schools, colleges, and even government organizations to put programs in place to foster healthy video gaming. Many of these programs can put an emphasis on education and learning in a healthy way.

Harvard's Business Journal published a report in 2011 about the importance of "Small Wins" throughout student learning experiences. The research shows that the most important factor in boosting emotion and motivation during the learning process was simply the feeling of "progress in meaningful work." Most video games are built around progress through the game with a series of small wins that lead toward a final goal. While parental and educational guidance is necessary in most cases in order to ensure positive educational value, the importance that students place on the "small wins" they gain from video games can translate into long term positive motivation to learn.

The Positive Impacts of Video Games

Hand-Eye Coordination
Playing video games can help players develop better hand-eye coordination and fine motor skills.

Analysis and Logic
Video games improve players' level of adeptness for pattern-recognition, analytical thinking, and problem-solving. Gamers can learn to think beyond the immediate facts of a situation, and instead consider the far-reaching implications of their choices (Schrier, 2018).

Better Spatial Awareness and Situational Awareness
In fighting games especially, players have to run, shoot and keep an eye on enemy positions, all at the same time. Games like this improve spatial skill and situational awareness.

Economic Management
Many multiplayer online game environments have an economic component that is complete with its own currency, virtual goods, and services. This can include economic changes like we see in the real world. In order to win games, players must exhibit economic intelligence to manage multiple economies efficiently. This is a skill that is easily transferred into real life ("10 Ways Multiplayer Gaming Economies Reflect Real-World Economy," 2018).

Logistics

Games such as those that mimic actual city planning and transportation systems have been credited with inspiring many people to pursue a career as a professional urban planner ("Must Reads: From video game to day job: How 'SimCity' inspired a generation of city planners—Los Angeles Times," n.d.).

Teamwork
Video games that are team-based improve players' ability to work cooperatively toward common objectives. Players learn to identify their strengths, build synergies, take responsibility, show initiative and demonstrate leadership. Useful levels of competition and teamwork teach players to pull their own weight within a group (read, 2017).

Problem Solving and Strategy
Video games teach players how to tackle immediate problems while keeping long-term objectives in mind. Instead of reacting impulsively to unfolding situations, players have to think many steps ahead. They not only have to plan their own moves, they must also anticipate and counter what the enemy does ("Playing Video Games Can Boost Fast Thinking," n.d.).

Quick-Thinking and Accuracy
There are so many variables in gaming environments. Players are expected to make split-second decisions in the midst of rapidly shifting dynamics. This hones players' abilities to think on their feet and greatly increases their capacity for quick analyses, fast decision-making, and decisiveness. These are the same abilities that are required by a surgeon ("Video Games Lead to Faster Decisions that are No Less Accurate," n.d.).

Many More...
These are just the tip of the iceberg when it comes to the benefits that can be derived from playing video games.

Surprising Uses for Video Games in Education and Learning
The "Gamification" of many industries is a new development that is closely following esports' push into the mainstream. One of the areas where this new trend is catching on fast is in education. This development is evident across a wide range of industries where people need to be trained for a variety of roles, to help businesses adapt their go-to-market strategies.

Teaching Children with Autism/ADHD
Minecraft has proven particularly effective for calming children with ADHD ("What My Son with ADHD Taught Me About Minecraft and Executive Functioning," 2016) (Sohn, 2014).

Learning English
A game-based English-as-a-Second Language (ESL) course found students learned better than by using traditional methods (Baierschmidt, n.d.).

Teaching Statistics
Stanford Graduate School of Education is using a modified version of the video game Space Invaders to improve students' understanding of statistics (University, Stanford, & California 94305, 2014).

Medical Training
Helping people develop a heightened sensitivity to their surroundings, video games are being used to train surgeons ("Video Games Lead to Faster Decisions that are No Less Accurate," n.d.).

Combat Readiness
The US military is using video games to improve soldiers' situational awareness ("Military Video Games Used to Train Troops on the Battlefield," 2017).

Strategies for Helping Young People Make the Most of Video Games

Finding a balance between the educational aspects in video games and the purely entertainment-driven side can be a challenge. Naturally, parents want to encourage educational experiences for their children. The approach some parents take of demonizing video games and banning kids from playing can be ineffective in most cases. Many parents have found that young people are resentful when parents cannot find common ground to accept video games as an educational or purely entertainment-driven portion of their lives. After reading this book, you should have a better understanding of how important esports already is for many young people around the world. In this section, you will learn productive strategies to help young people get the most educational value out of video games (CNN, n.d.).

As you may imagine, helping young people get educational value from video games can require an involved approach on the part of parents and educators. Unlike traditional sports, many parents today do not understand gaming the way that their children do. Many parents do not share their children's enthusiasm for esports. Consequently, parents are sometimes unable to serve as a regulating influence on the way young people consume video games. In order to be a positive influence on their children's' use of video games, parents must find common ground. It is almost impossible to help a young person manage video games properly without some understanding of the culture surrounding video games ("How to Handle Your Child's Video Game Obsession Positively," 2015).

Below are important ways parents and coaches can help young people derive educational value out of the time they spend playing video games.

Why Video Games Are So Alluring

Adults need to understand that video games are so compelling for young people because they tap into a source of wonder and excitement. Most children and teenagers are at a stage in their lives where they are learning how the world works. Children and teens engage in games because they offer a chance to gain mastery over their fears in a safe environment. While parents may think of video games as a waste of time, the gamer views it as an exciting experiential learning process (Olson, 2010).

Some of the key elements of games that make them so compelling include:

Challenge

The chance to confront a seemingly insurmountable situation, think a problem through, and implement a solution is challenging. Gamers experience pride as they accomplish challenging goals. Winning in a video game often translates to a young person exhibiting confidence to tackle real-life problems.

Growth

Learning via video gaming is similar to how humans in a natural setting learn. The lessons taught via video games are often acquired through curiosity, discovery, and participation. Many students find this style of learning more engaging than the traditional lectures they are used to at school. Therefore, video games are almost never boring. Good video game experiences supply a seemingly endless supply of new information.

Status

Video games, like traditional sports, give young people the chance to gain the respect of their peers. Many gamers develop the feeling of becoming an important member of their tribe. Adults may not understand it, but young people use games to feel more accepted in the world around them.

Risk Within A Controlled Environment

Airline pilots use flight simulators to learn how to fly. Similarly, young people use video games to learn otherwise foreign concepts. Without flight simulators, becoming a licensed pilot would be a much more life-threatening affair. How would they learn to handle an aircraft in stormy weather?

Fantasy

Our creativity is linked to our imagination. Video games unshackle the mind from the limits of reality and allow us to wander. The creative process begins with the ability to think outside the limits of what is ordinary or accepted. Video games not only enhance the freedom to think, but they also give our imagination structure that lets our brain grasp elusive concepts (S. University, 2013).

Engagement and Exertion

School learning is often a model in passivity. Games provide opportunities for young people to work hard at something that they choose by themselves. They learn to focus, be persistent and use critical thinking skills during video games. All of this happens while gamers learn to be tolerant of failure. The gaming experience allows gamers the ability to mentally undertake and complete difficult tasks.

Regulating Feelings

Kids often play video games as an outlet for negative emotions. Video games give young people a safe space to be rebellious and mischievous without getting into trouble. Kids use video games to help cope with anger, stress, and loneliness (R & Kulman, 2014). When adults understand young peoples' gaming habits, they may begin to see things from a different perspective. Adults and educators who carefully study video games can use strategies to help children navigate the world of esports more effectively.

Developing a Video Gaming Management Strategy

In general, video games can be divided into two broad categories:

Educational Video Games

These are video games that are specifically created with education in mind. They include games like **Be Trapped** and **WordSearch Deluxe** (word puzzle games), **Chicken Invaders 2** (The solar system), **Twelve A Dozen** (Algebra), **Logical Journey of the Zoombinis** (Logic), **SimCell** (Science), and **Mighty Math's Cosmic Geometry** (Simple Arithmetic and Geometry). Games developed by these companies - Big Fish Games, Amplify Learning, Broderbund, and Educational Insights - are usually educational.

Non-Educational Video Games with Educational Elements

These are games which, although not designed to teach school subjects like the previous category, can still impart various skills to the players. Examples include management games, which entail raising and managing funds, as well as dealing with business competitors (The Zoo and Simcity), role-playing games that teach map-reading and decision-making (World of Warcraft and Tomb Raider), and strategy games, which offer lessons in real history, experimentation, teamwork, and discovery (Flight Simulator X, Age of Empires, and Empire Earth).

In addition to the above, video games can teach non-cognitive skills, such as patience and discipline, which have a more direct correlation to success in life than IQ. If used properly, games can be a powerful tool for supplementing classroom learning ("Are Video Games Educational?," n.d.). By and large, the only way to know the educational value of a game is to research it and most importantly, play it. Here is an outline of things parents and educators can do to jumpstart the process of helping young people learn through video games.

Play The Games
This is an indispensable step to helping kids learn through gaming. Playing games with children is a key way to position adults as an ally in the child's mind. However, due to the many constraints of adult life, always being available at game-time may not be feasible. Given this, in addition to playing the games online, you can recruit relatives and trusted friends to play with children ("Get Over Yourself and Play Video Games With Your Kid," n.d.).

Be A Student
Creating a safe space for children to talk about their gameplay is important. Creating common ground where parents and coaches can be spectators during gameplay, can give adults a chance to become a part of their gaming experience, even when they are not actively participating. After all, how many soccer moms actually play soccer? By allowing the child to "school you" in the game, you can learn about it and can regulate their game time more effectively ("8 Reasons Video Games Can Improve Your Child," n.d.).

Schedule Game Time
The time that kids play a game matter. It is not advisable for children to start off playing video games in the morning. Also, gaming should generally be limited during school days. Some parents report that once children get into game mode, they find it hard to switch back into their school routine.

Finally, gaming should be reserved for after activities you want the children to participate in.

Create Gaming Objectives

Many of the video games today can help children learn specific lessons. Game developers have often found fun and exciting ways for gamers to accomplish objectives. Children often focus on the fun part, but adults can help gamers learn more by working to create goals and design plans to reach them.

Take It Beyond Game Time

Many games demand that players do some thinking away from the screen. For example, in Simcity, to lay tracks for a railway needed to expand your city, you must learn how to plan out a city. This can require actual research. Similarly, you need economics to win many of the strategy and multiplayer online battle arena games. Educators can also deliberately seek out ways for students to employ game concepts in the classroom.

Make It Serious Business

Depending on the game being played, the player can journal about their gaming experience. This process would involve documenting objectives, defining a clear strategy, identifying reasons for failures to meet objectives, and new approaches to solving challenges. This introduces structured thinking, planning, and writing into the gaming activity. This can help transform what was previously just a fun activity into a well-thought-out process.

Create Competition

Gaming can often be about competition. Competition often allows players to derive their greatest amount of pride from the activity of gaming. Competing against one another or side-by-side builds relationships. It also provides a platform for teaching, as adults can meld kids' gaming expertise to their real-world experience, in order to devise a strategy.

Ask Questions

Challenge student thinking by critiquing their game choices. Parents and educators can provide different perspectives on the decision's gamers make. For younger children, you can use questions to encourage problem-solving and further learning. For teenagers, the discussions could serve as touchpoints for discussing real-world problems and educational subjects (Shapiro, n.d.).

6 FROM TEENAGE PASTIME TO THE INTERNATIONAL STAGE

Esports has come a very long way from the inconspicuous beginnings of October 1972, when Stanford Artificial Intelligence Lab (Los Altos, California) hosted the first-ever competitive video game event. What used to be viewed as a teenage obsession, reserved for adolescents who had a hard time making friends in real life (at least, in parents' view) has morphed into an international phenomenon. Esports now has the potential to disrupt and irreversibly alter the way we create and consume competitive sports (Baker & Baker, 2016).

Today, esports is already a multibillion-dollar industry. It is growing at a pace never seen before in the history of all sports. Milestones that have taken global sports like basketball, baseball, football, soccer, and tennis the better part of the last century to achieve, will be reached and eclipsed by esports before the first quarter of this century is over. Just last year a 16-year-old Fortnite player won more than Tiger Woods at the Master's golf tournament. Yet, a recent report shows that most adults over the age of 35 do not know that this is happening. While teenage video game heroes are making more than the world's top golf and tennis players, only two out of ten adults past the age of 35 know that esports exist ("The Global Games Market Will Generate $152.1 Billion in 2019 as the U.S. Overtakes China as the Biggest Market | Newzoo," n.d.).

What is Esports?

According to Wikipedia, "Esports is a form of competitive sports using video games." This definition lives on the internet, where there are no clear distinctions between "real sports" and "Esports." Esports has come quite a long way since Espen Aarseth published her first issue of *Computer Game Studies*. If you are a "Digital Native" you are already familiar with gaming culture and esports. Digital natives are generally born after the 1980s and they are considered by historians as "Generation Y." This is a generation considered to be comfortable with technology in the "digital age" because they have grown up surrounded by a world full of computers, smartphones, and other internet-connected devices.

If you are a "Digital Migrant" you were born before the 1980s. The term characterizes those who are generally fearful about using technology.

Disregarding these general stereotypes, to understand esports today, you must discard any outdated concepts of video games that are played with friends in a single home. Esports today is born from an interconnected world of online video gaming. Video games today are now part of a fully immersive and highly interactive world that generations of gamers engage with.

Esports games encompass highly organized multiplayer competitions between amateur and professional teams. This billion-dollar industry now includes many things we associate with "real sports" including professional athletes with yearly contracts, endorsement deals, and fan stardom. Yes, this also includes huge stadiums packed with fans and millions of online viewers. Yes, this includes professional leagues, mega-sponsorship deals, and year-round competitions attracting contestants from around the world. Consider the world of sports that you grew up with and imagine if everyone you knew at school could play the sport you are interested in learning from home. Imagine how much more engaged you would be with your favorite sport if you could play baseball in your living room? Imagine how many more of your friends growing up would have joined the baseball team if they didn't have to leave home to do so.

The following events are a highly compressed timeline of the development of esports.

- **1972**: The "Intergalactic Spacewar Olympics" is hosted by Stanford University. The winner received a one-year subscription of Rolling Stone magazine and title of "Intergalactic *Spacewar* Champion" for 1972.
- **1980**: The first large-scale video game tournament, with 10,000 participants in attendance, was held in New York by Atari, marking the entrance of competitive gaming into the mainstream ("History of Esports," n.d.).
- **1982**: The show *Starcade,* an esports program, makes its debut on television. 133 episodes are aired from 1982 to 1984.
- **1988**: The modern era of online gaming is birthed with the first team-based internet game, Netrek.
- **1990**: The 1990 Nintendo World Championships. After touring the United States, this tournament has its grand finale at Universal Studios Hollywood (California).
- **1993**: Netrek is attracting record numbers of up to 5,000 players daily.

- **1994**: Nintendo PowerFest '94", the Nintendo 2nd World Championship for the Super Nintendo Entertainment System is held in San Diego, California.
- **1997**: Red Annihilation Tournament, the first global esports event, has a grand prize of a 1987 Ferrari 328 GTS belonging to the lead developer of the game.
- **1997**: The Cyberathlete Professional League is born. The CPL tournament follows in 1998 with $15,000 prize money.
- **2005**: The CPL World Tour, a year-long international competition, spanning nine countries on four continents, has a total prize pool of $1,000,000.
- **2005**: The creation of YouTube as a video-sharing platform gives millions of ordinary people the ability to easily share and watch videos online. YouTube's dedicated gaming service *YouTube Gaming* accelerates the esports revolution.
- **2011**: Twitch enters as a dedicated video-game live-streaming platform, including broadcasts of esports competitions. Before its acquisition by Amazon (2014), it had received 45 million unique viewers and ranked 4ᵗʰ in peak Internet traffic in the USA, after Netflix, Apple and Google.
- **2012 - 2016**: The video gaming market is recognized as the fastest-growing entertainment industry in the world, with sustained year-on-year growth of 6% in 2012 (Lee - & Tzialli, n.d.).
- **2014**: 45,000 in-person attendees at Sangam Stadium (Seoul) for the League of Legends World Final and over 27 million watching online.
- **2016**: TBS and ESPN start to invest in esports leagues, as well as broadcasting competitions.
- **2016**: The first franchised league, the Overwatch League, by Blizzard Entertainment, starts, initially with twelve teams and twenty currently.
- **2016**: From meager rewards players earned initially, prizes reach jaw-dropping amounts: Dota2 (US $86 million) and League of Legends ($30 million). In 2018, *The International* broke the record with a $25 million prize pool for a single tournament.
- **2017**: The number of esports viewers tripled from around 100 million (2012) to over 300 million (2017) ("The Rise of Esports," 2018).
- **2017**: The League of Legends World Final in Beijing was viewed by 60 million people.

- **2018**: The NBA, in partnership with Take-Two Interactive, creates NBA 2K League, the first esports league run by a professional sports league.
- **2018**: Revenue from the global esports industry hits $905 million and is expected to exceed $1 billion in two years. Over 50% of revenue to come from China and North America ("The explosive growth of Esports," n.d.).
- **2018**: In 2018, the highest-earning esports teams receive $23,987,734.23 (Team Liquid), $20,696,040.79 (Evil Geniuses), and $17,562,308.50 (Team OG).
- **2019**: Gamers across the world expected to spend $152.1 billion on games in 2019, ("The Global Games Market Will Generate $152.1 Billion in 2019 as the U.S. Overtakes China as the Biggest Market | Newzoo," n.d.).
- **2019**: Esports' highest-earning player, Kuro Takhamosi, has earned $4,097,926.95 to date.
- **2022**: Esports billed to be included as a medal event in the Asian Games.
- **2024**: The International Olympic Committee (IOC) is considering a decision to include Esports as a demonstration sport.

Before the arrival of online gaming, video game systems were designed primarily for one to four players in the same location. The user-interface or game controllers were usually gamepads or joysticks designed for in-room play. The output from the gaming console was designed for televisions of the time but they lacked connectivity. These systems were technically "offline" and they were limited to gameplay with gamers being in direct contact with the equipment ("Video game," 2019).

Online gaming, on the other hand, permits players to break out of these limitations by allowing people who are physically separated to interact within the same game environment. An online gaming system is made up of a system of computers linked together via the internet or a local area network. Each computer has a version of the game installed and players can log into an online server to play games with others from around the world. This allows players to view the actions of other players over the network. Players can now make moves of their own to counter what others are doing. All of this is rendered in real-time to give players the sense of being in the same shared space. These are real people, playing really intricate, fast-paced games. With online video gaming players always have a friend they can play with. The engagement makes playing against computer-controlled opponents pale in comparison.

7 WHAT IS DRIVING THE ESPORTS PHENOMENON?

Competition is the driving motivation for athletes. Competition pushes players to work on the skills that are essential to winning. This passion to be the best in esports has proven to draw large audiences of fans to the sport. For esports, the leap from peripheral gaming to globally recognized competitions is driven mostly by breakthroughs in technology and athlete passion for the game. Esports could not exist without its supporting technology infrastructure. Now that the required infrastructure is in place throughout most developed countries, the growth of this sport will be phenomenal. Every year the barriers to entry continue to decrease, as technology gets better and more affordable.

In addition to the elements already mentioned, the esports phenomenon is supported by game developers who continue to create new and exciting games. Game developers are now studying the gamer and their fans who are watching online. By making video games fun to watch, developers can evangelize the spread of their creations through the eyes of millions of online fans.

An Intersection of Technologies

Over the last twenty years, there have been specific technological events that have enabled the rise in the popularity of esports.

Advanced Video Games/Hardware
- Player Versus Player modes in games let players compete against one another instead of competing against a computer. Online ranking systems and player interactions have been key developments in esports.
- Full two-way communications using voice and chat have opened up new levels of cooperation in multiplayer gaming. Increased interaction with online audiences has developed with players live streaming their gameplay to services such as Twitch™. High levels of interactivity between players, games, and audiences is a key differentiator in esports versus traditional sports.

- More affordable gear for gaming, which includes computers, monitors, headsets, and graphics cards reduce barriers to entry into competitive gaming. As economies of scale push the price of video gaming hardware down, more people around the world can afford to play.
- Cloud-based gaming ecosystems are just now starting to remove barriers to entry in a big way. Google Stadia, for example, puts the power of the cloud into the hands of anyone for just $129 currently. Cloud-based gaming is putting big-budget games into the hands of millions without the need for expensive consoles.

Internet Speed

The most important part of the online gaming ecosystem has always been an internet connection that links players around the world. Until the last decade, most internet speeds have not been fast enough to permit online gaming at a grand scale. Gaming consumes a lot of bandwidth and with poor connections, there is too much lag to play competitive games. Poor internet affects player performance and spectators' ability to watch the games. Esports contests are often decided in milliseconds and a network with too much latency interferes with players' ability to respond within the game environment competitively ("r/explainlikeimfive - ELI5," n.d.).

Live Streaming

Live streaming is one of the important factors that has unleashed the full potential of online gaming as a spectator sport. Live streaming has made it possible for millions of gaming enthusiasts to arrange themselves into tribes, behind their favorite players and games. YouTube Gaming, Twitch, and Mixer have given players a platform where they can show off their gameplay, as well as build credibility and followings. Spectators also use these platforms to watch esports replays of their favorite players on-demand. In 2019 alone Twitch has already logged an astounding 560 billion total minutes of viewership. Twitch currently ranks ahead of Cable TV networks for the volume of viewers ("The rise of Esports as a spectator phenomenon," 2018).

Multiplayer Video Games

Multiplayer games have allowed players to interact in the same game environment in a way that used to be impossible. Individual players can compete against other players to hone their skills against players who rank at the top of their class. Players can build teams, share objectives, and even supervise one another's play. This has allowed social systems built upon rivalries, status, partnerships, and shared goals to emerge within the game worlds. These virtual social systems spill over into the real world to create loyalties among fans and allow the best players to build tribes of followers (Selk, politics, elections, n.d.).

Spectators

Perhaps the biggest constraint faced by esports is the barrier to entry gaming can require in comparisons to traditional sports like soccer or basketball. In soccer, for example, kids only need a ball and space around the neighborhood to play. To play video games and compete competitively, one must buy hardware, which can often need upgrading to compete in the top ranks. Since most spectators only watch sports that they have played themselves before, this has been an issue for growth in the sport. However, with the widespread adoption of a free-to-play video game model by most modern game developers, this problem has been solved for the most part.

With growing numbers of people who play casually, the stage has been set for online gaming to become a spectator sport for the masses. Current estimates say that up to 40% of those who watch esports have never played the games they watch. The percentage of esports spectators who do not actively play the video game they are watching is expected to grow over the next decade. Cloud-based gaming, which will be discussed more in a later chapter, will further reduce barriers to entry along with increasingly powerful and affordable mobile phone technology. ("Breaking Down The Incredible Rise Of Esports | Benzinga," n.d.) ("Global Esports viewership by viewer type 2022," n.d.).

Competition

Team-based gaming, large prizes, sponsorships, scholarships, and live streaming are all driving the competitive nature of esports. Previously, players could only compete against computer-generated opponents in the gaming environment. Being able to play against other humans allows players to rank themselves against rival players. Additionally, when players stream their play to Twitch or YouTube, they start to acquire a reputation that allows them to build a loyal fan base. Loyal fans will naturally create rivalries with fans of other players. Tournaments then become proving grounds for top-ranking players where fans can get excited in the same way the NFL super-bowl draws fans every year.

Tournaments

With the spectator and competition aspects of the esports equation accounted for, it was only a matter of time before tournaments would follow. Tournaments are a natural result of competition and increasing spectator interest. Brand sponsorships in esports now include corporate heavyweights like Coca-Cola, PepsiCo, Gillette, Audi, Bud Light, and many more. Existing esports tournaments will only get bigger with time, and new ones are to be expected every year. FIFA (Fédération Internationale de Football Association) already has an eWorld Cup and other sporting federations are hashing out plans to create an esports version of their established sports ("The explosive growth of Esports," n.d.).

8 TYPES OF ESPORTS

Although there are many types of games included under the umbrella of esports, each one can be classified under a specific category based on the type of gameplay. The same way combat sports are classified based on disciplines, esports are categorized by the form of play within the game ("What Are The Game Types?," n.d.).

Esports are divided into the following categories:

Player vs. Player (PvP) Games

This is one of the oldest formats in video games. Player versus Player, or "PvP" games, involve one player squaring off against another player, or a group of players, in the typical fight scenario. The earliest esports tournaments were mostly based on fighting games and were styled after popular arcade games (Programs, n.d.).

Examples:

- **Super Smash Brothers**: This is one of the most successful games in the fighting genre. It has been featured in many high-profile international tournaments. Super Smash Brothers was originally released by Nintendo in 1999. This popular fighting game features many of the classic Nintendo characters including Mario, Luigi, Link, Samus, and Pikachu.

- **Mortal Kombat**: This is arguably one of the most popular one-on-one combat games. Mortal Kombat was originally released in 1992 and has a reputation for having high levels of violent content, including "Fatalities" which were finishing moves that could be used to defeat an opponent.

First-Person Shooter (FPS) Games

In first-person shooter games, each player views the game through the eyes of the character they are controlling. While gamers can generally choose to view their character in a third-person view, the first-person view is required for instantaneous reaction times. Games under this category are very popular in esports competitions ("List of Esports games," 2019).

Examples:

    · **Call of Duty**: Call of Duty is a popular first-person shooter game, especially in North America. This game was originally set during the Second World War. More recent versions of the game are set in modern times, in the midst of the cold war and even futuristic worlds.

    · **Overwatch**: Overwatch is the official game of one of the biggest esports leagues in the world. The Overwatch League features professional players with regular salaries. The game is set in a near-future world where two teams of six battle for victory.

    · **Counter-Strike**: This game is consistently featured in competitions in Europe and America. Counter-Strike is part of the million-dollar competition called the Eleague major. In this game, one team acts as terrorists who plan to perpetrate an act of terror and the opposing team acts as counter-terrorists trying to prevent the act.

    · **Fortnite**: Fortnite is a "battle royale" style first-person shooter game. Fortnite battles feature 100 players on a single map that decreases in size until there is only one winner left. Fortnite can be played in solo, duo or squad modes.

Real-time Strategy (RTS) Games
These games are the chess of esports. They are team-based and involve deep levels of strategy to win. Rival teams compete for control of resources they can use to defeat their opponent. The emphasis is on managing resources to defeat rivals.

Examples:

    · **Civilization Series:** Civilization is a turn-based strategy game that allows players to build civilizations from prehistory to modern times. This strategy game allows players to build and improve cities. Players are encouraged to "Explore, Expand, Exploit and Exterminate" in order to win. Players can choose to research new technologies and make cultural, intellectual, and technical decisions to influence the growth of their civilization.

- **XCOM 2:** XCOM 2 is a turn-based tactics video game that allows players to build military organizations to fight off an alien invasion. Players can command squad members in battles against their enemies and make decisions on how to build their force.

- **Hearthstone:** Hearthstone is a free-to-play strategy card game that is based on the rich history of Warcraft. This type of turned-based card game has been popular for many years. Other popular card games of this type include Magic the Gathering and Pokémon.

Multiplayer Online Battle Arena (MOBA) Games

Players in multiplayer online battle arenas focus on teamwork to win. Most MOBA games have small groups of teams that compete against each other to win. Teams will use headsets to communicate in real-time during gameplay. The biggest esports tournaments are under this category ("Types of E-sports games," 2018).

Examples:

- **Defense of the Ancients 2 (DOTA2):** DOTA2 is played with two teams of five players, each occupying and defending a team base. Each of the 10 players independently controls their own "hero" who features unique abilities that can be used to further the team's efforts. From 2013 up to the present, the annual DOTA2 tournament, The International, has had some of the largest prize pools in the history of esports. It was $2.8 million in 2013 and $34 million in 2019.

- **League of Legends (LoL):** League of Legends is a multiplayer game similar to DOTA2, where players compete in matches to destroy the opposing team's "Nexus" or base. Players compete in matches that can last anywhere from 20 to 60 minutes on average. LoL is popular all over the world and similar to DOTA2 tournaments have been posting amazing prizes. The 2017 League of Legends final was viewed by 60 million people.

Sports Simulation Games

These are esports replicas of traditional sports. They are designed to mimic the sports they are modeled after. Their only difference is usually that they are played on an electronic device versus a field, court, ring, or racetrack.

The Center for Educational Innovation is currently combining sports simulation games with real-world sports activities. They have found this as an effective strategy for encouraging real-world action outside of video game interest with students. Sports simulation games now require enough skill and gaming mechanics to be considered their own competitive sports.

Examples

·   FIFA Series, NBA2K, Madden NFL, as well as various forms of car racing games.

·   NBA2K launched a very successful league in 2017 and now has 21 active teams.

9 TOP ESPORTS TOURNAMENTS

What are the top esports tournaments in the world? How many people are participating? Who are the organizers? In this section of the book, there is an outline of the top professional tournaments, along with a review of the organizations helping to create leagues at the high school and college levels.

Worldwide

The International

The 2019 International, a DOTA2 championship held in Shanghai, China happened in August 2019. There were 18 teams from around the world and 90 players in the event. The total prize pool was more than $30 million dollars. The tournament was organized and sponsored by Valve Corporation, a company based in Seattle and the owners of DOTA2. The event venue, the Mercedes-Benz Arena, has 18,000 seats that were sold out. During the grand finals, 1.1 million people viewed the event on Twitch ("The International 2019—Liquipedia Dota 2 Wiki," n.d.).

Fortnite World Cup

The Fortnite World Cup Finals have two events. A solo event and a duo event. Both events had prize pools of over $15 million each. Each final had 100 players competing and the event occurred in July of 2019 in New York City. Fortnite is organized by an American video and software development company, Epic Games, Inc. The tournament venue was a 23,700-person capacity stadium, which was also totally sold out. A total of 2.3 million people viewed it online ("A 16-year-old just won $3M playing in the Fortnite World Cup—CNET," n.d.).

Counter-Strike: Global Offensive Major Tournaments

These competitions are generally rated as the most important CS:GO tournaments in the world. They are organized by Valve Corporation, developers of the game, and they are held twice a year. Usually, there are 24 teams competing from four regions in the world; Americas, Asia, CIS, and Europe. The prize pool is in the $1 million range. The latest edition of the competition was held between August and September of 2019 ("The Ins and Outs of CS:GO Tournaments: 2016–2018—DreamTeam Blog," n.d.).

Overwatch World Cup

The Overwatch World Cup is related to the Overwatch League and often has the same players as the league. However, players in the World Cup represent their countries, rather than their professional teams and organizations, as they do in the league. In the Overwatch World Cup, teams do not compete for money, but all teams receive the same prize of $16,000. This twist makes it one of the most interesting international esports tournaments ("The Overwatch League |—Overwatch World Cup," n.d.).

North America

Evolution Championship Series (USA)
This event happened in August of 2019 in Las Vegas, Nevada. Attendance was reportedly greater than 9,000. The total prize pool was $254,289 ("Evo 2020 Championship Series | Official Website of the Evolution 2020 World Championship Series," n.d., p. 202).

Capcom Cup (USA)
The final event of the Capcom Pro Tour is a series of fighting game tournaments organized by Capcom. The prize pool was $250,000 in the last tournament ("Capcom Pro Tour 2019 Full Schedule and Details Reveal | Capcom Pro Tour," n.d.).

Halo World Championship Series
Sponsored by Microsoft, the Halo Championship series takes place annually, with multiple events across cities in the United States ("HCS Invitational 2019—Halo Esports Wiki," n.d.).

Asia

League of Legends Champions Korea
The LCK is the primary route for South Korean esports teams to progress to the League of Legends World Championship. It is organized by Riot Games in partnership with various sponsors ("LCK 2019 Spring—Leaguepedia | League of Legends Esports Wiki," n.d.).

Global Starcraft II League (South Korea)
The GSL is a tournament-based league in South Korea that features a long list of competitions held year-round. The GSL is hosted by Afreeca TV, GSL, and Blizzard entertainment ("Global StarCraft II League—Liquipedia—The StarCraft II Encyclopedia," n.d.).

League of Legends Pro League (China)

This is the top League of Legends league in China and the primary qualification route for Chinese esports teams looking to compete in the League of Legends World Championship ("LoL Pro League—Liquipedia League of Legends Wiki," n.d.).

PUBG Mobile India Series

PUBG Mobile India Series is a premier mobile series in India. The event is massive in scale, attracting over half a million registrations, with up to 400,000 rounds played during the course of the tournament (Gaming, n.d.).

League of Legends India Champions Cup

This is India's premier League of Legends league. The top teams from this tournament get a chance to qualify for the League of Legends World Championships.

Europe

DreamHack (Sweden)

DreamHack is the world's largest computer festival. This festival also includes an esports tournament by the same name. It boasts the fastest internet and LAN connections in the world ("DreamHack – World of Gamers · Community of Friends," n.d.).

GameBattles UK

This is a huge competition in esports, featuring a variety of games and some of the largest prize pools in Europe ("GameBattles: The World Leader in Online Video Game Competition," n.d.).

Other Regions

- Cybergamer (Oceania)

- eXTREMESLAND (Oceania, Middle-East, Asia)

- Mind Sports South Africa

Professional Esports Leagues

The Overwatch League (OWL)

OWL is the official league for the first-person shooter game Overwatch by Blizzard-Activision. It holds the record for the highest number of hours viewed by any esports league. The league is organized into stages that last four to five weeks with 28 matches played. Each stage is concluded with a tournament where the stage champion is crowned. The total prize pool for the league is $5 million.

League of Legends World Championship
This is the concluding event for the year-long season of League of Legends. The event lasts for a full month and the prize pools are expected to grow to over 2 million USD as the competition progresses. Twenty-four teams representing thirteen regions will be competing at the events. The tournament is organized by Riot Games (USA) a company of Tencent Holdings Limited, China ("2019 World Championship—Liquipedia League of Legends Wiki," n.d.).

Call of Duty World League
This tournament is organized by Activision and Treyarch. In 2019, they hosted the seventh edition of the annual Call of Duty Championship. It is held in Los Angeles, California with thirty-two teams in attendance. The total prize pool was $2 million and the event was sponsored by ASUS, Scuf Gaming, ASTRO Gaming, and Mountain Dew ("Call of Duty World League Championship 2019—Call of Duty Esports Wiki," n.d.).

Esports Leagues in North America

With the growing popularity of esports and its unstoppable encroachment into the world of traditional sports, it was only a matter of time before esports began to take the shape and structure of organized sports. This is already happening with the creation of esports leagues in the amateur, professional, state, and national levels. Below is a sample of the leagues that are helping to push esports deeper into the fabrics of our educational systems and entertainment industries.

High School Esports Leagues

PlayVS + NFHS
PlayVS became the recognized high school esports league after they entered a partnership with the National Federation of State High School Associations (NFHS). This partnership will allow PlayVS to set up esports programs in high schools across the United States. This means high schools now have a regular-season of esports, just as they have for other categories of sports. This will enable students to compete in officially recognized esports tournaments, with the possibility of earning university scholarships ("PlayVS | The Official High School Esports League," n.d.).

High School Esports League (HSEL)

HSEL is the largest and oldest high school esports league in Canada and the USA. The HSEL has a rich offering of esports programs. Students can participate in HSEL knowing that they are engaging in a legitimate varsity sport. The HSEL recently entered a strategic partnership with the Varsity Esports Foundation (VESF) to facilitate its goals of financing league fees, providing gaming equipment, and helping exceptional cyber-athletes secure university scholarships ("High School Esports League Compete for Esports Glory," n.d.).

Electronic Gaming Federation (EFGH)

The EFGH is the premier state-endorsed national esports league in the USA. It organizes two annual esports championships at the state and national levels. It also works with schools to develop their esports programs and via the EFGH. The EFGH acts as a governing body for collegiate and high school esports leagues. This program covers only esports leagues which have been endorsed by the education authorities ("Home," n.d.) .

Other High School Leagues

Included are: North American Scholastic Esports Federation, Legacy Esports, as well as many state-level Esports leagues.

College Esports League and Programs

National Association of Collegiate Esports (NACE)

This is the umbrella body for college and university esports programs. NACE currently has more than sixty recognized programs from colleges and universities across the USA. It is a member-based organization that puts a strong emphasis on esports scholarships as an instrument for driving varsity esports development. NACE actively works with colleges and universities to start their own esports programs ("Home—Collegiate Esports Governing Body," n.d.).

Below is a list of five universities that are currently viewed as having some of the best esports programs. The list is based on a school's success in tournaments, how much they have invested in their esports infrastructure, the quality of their esports scholarships, and the depth of their academic programs (Writers, 2018).

Maryville University of Saint Louis (Town and Country, MO)

Winner of the 2016 League of Legends Championship, Maryville University of Saint Louis holds the record for an unbeaten run of 40 wins in the Collegiate Star League of 2017.

Robert Morris University Illinois (Chicago, IL)

By offering a scholarship to the university's League of Legends team in 2014, long before other programs offered scholarships, Robert Morris University of Illinois became a pioneer in varsity esports. Their partnership with major corporations has helped build one of the best esports facilities in the United States.

Miami University (Oxford, OH)
Winner of the National Association of Collegiate Esports (NACE) Overwatch season (2017) and runner-up at the NACE League of Legends invitational for 2017, the school's esports scholarship program was created in 2016.

University of California-Irvine (Irvine, CA)
The University of California-Irvine was the first public university to create an esports team. The University boasts a top-notch facility located right outside Los Angeles. The school's esports scholarship program is ahead in terms of the scholarship amounts offered and the quality of its academic programs.

University of Utah (Salt Lake City, UT)
The University of Utah has one of the most comprehensive esports programs in the United States. The University offers an undergraduate degree in gaming and game development programs. It also has one of the largest scholarship programs in varsity esports.

10 COLLEGE LEVEL ESPORTS PROGRAMS

Established colleges and universities are now starting to offer esports programs across the United States and the world. Today, there are more than 125 varsity level esports programs registered with the national governing body NACE (National Association of Collegiate Esports). Educational organizations that have long been on the spectator side of online gaming are now becoming hubs for innovation in esports. Schools are starting to offer scholarships for excellence in esports to attract the talent they need to build teams that can compete on a national stage.

In an earlier chapter, you learned that several universities now have standard esports teams participating in league-based tournaments and competitions. Many of these educational institutions are introducing new programs and facilities to help prepare the next generation of students to pursue careers in the esports industry. In this chapter, you will gain a glimpse into some of the most successful programs established over the past couple of years.

Varsity Esports

Harrisburg University (Pennsylvania)
Harrisburg University is a private STEM-focused school located in the Pennsylvania state capital city of Harrisburg. It was founded in 2001 and places an emphasis on Science, Technology, Engineering, and Mathematics. Harrisburg University has made national headlines for the school's full-ride scholarships being offered to esports athletes. 22-year old Alex Carrell, a high-ranking Hearthstone player, left his school in Central Washington for a full-ride scholarship to Harrisburg University in 2019. In an age when college educations can be unaffordable, Carrell only has $40,000 worth of student debt left from his previous school in Washington. Being awarded a full scholarship for esports is certainly a life-changing opportunity.

Harrisburg University hosts an annual esports tournament called the "Harrisburg University Esports Invitational" where students compete against local esports teams. The school has a student population of only 750, making esports players a big deal for the campus culture. Harrisburg went 33-0 in their first season competing in the varsity Overwatch league. The school currently has 26 student-athletes, all of whom either play League of Legends, Overwatch, or Hearthstone competitively. The university has recruited former esports athlete Chad Smeltz as the head coach.

The Atlantic reports that "Schools like Harrisburg are playing an entirely different game [compared to most schools]... They are willing to treat college esports like Alabama treats college football" (Winkie, 2019). Such forward-thinking programs are helping educational institutions grow and attract new students.

Esports & Media

Newhouse School: Syracuse University (New York State)

In 2018, the prestigious Syracuse University put its 149 years of proud history behind the burgeoning esports industry. The University's Newhouse School, which has courses spanning every aspect of media and communication, has launched a new course called "Esports & Media." The course was launched in collaboration with Twitch, the world's largest esports streaming platform. According to the school, the course will give students a holistic view of the esports industry. It will incorporate a full history of esports' journey from obscurity into the multi-billion dollar industry that it is today ("Twitch Will Assist with New Newhouse Course in Esports and Media," n.d.).

The course hopes to be able to train students for a variety of esports careers at a rate that matches the industry's growth and demand for trained professionals. By partnering with Twitch, the university is ensuring that the course will stay on top of the trends in the industry. In fact, Twitch meets with the school regularly to remain relevant to what students need to thrive in the sector. Newhouse School has also said that the class will have its own dedicated channel on Twitch for live streaming. Twitch works closely with the school to arrange guests for shows that bring a live broadcast and streaming element to the curriculum.

Some of the content and intended outcomes of the course include:

· Giving students insight into the entrepreneurial side of the gaming industry.

· Guiding students to opportunities for making meaningful contributions to the online gaming scene.

· Helping students understand how esports intersects with media and broadcasting.

· Offering comprehensive lessons in the history of esports development.

· An examination of esports technologies and various business models in the industry.

· An in-depth look at the parts played by teams, leagues, tournaments, and streaming services.

· Provide opportunities for students to work directly with esports organizations in the production of original content.

HUB Esports Arena & Gaming Lounge

University of Washington (Seattle, WA.)

The University of Washington is taking a different approach to the convergence of esports and education. The University has recently completed and opened its first 1,000 square-foot gaming center. The facility makes the University of Washington the biggest public university to have a space that is entirely dedicated to esports. The idea behind the creation of the center is to serve as a meeting point between students of the university and companies in the gaming industry. It will also function as a nucleus for the university's gaming culture. Among other things, the facility is designed to host sponsored tournaments and generate income by offering gaming as a service. Students, faculty, and staff receive discounted rates but the facility is also open to the public for competitive hourly rates ("'More than just playing a game,'" 2019).

The University of Washington says it intends to use the hub as a bridge between its student communities and the 23,000 jobs in interactive media that are available in Seattle alone. By providing a space where professional esports events can be held, it hopes to take students experience of esports beyond casual gaming. The hub will give the University of Washington students and faculty a deeper level of exposure to esports. The space affords students direct access to esports companies and competitions all year round.

The University's HUB Esports Arena & Gaming Lounge will also serve as a platform for prominent esports personalities. These players, at the highest level of the industry, will be invited to speak to students and educate them about different aspects of gaming. By being open for casual gaming, it also gives students a chance to gauge their skill and interest levels. It is a space where students can evaluate their chances of a career in esports, either as athletes or on the business side. The hub is equipped with the following:

- 40 high-end gaming computers

- 2 VR (Virtual Reality) systems

- 1 broadcasting station to live stream on Twitch

- 23 Unlocked PC games

- 6 Unlocked VR games

Syracuse University, Harrisburg University, and the University of Washington are just three examples showing what the future of esports and education will hold. As educational institutions start to take steps to integrate their offerings with esports, they are forging a path for students to prepare for technical careers in this industry.

There is a common misconception from the public that the esports industry can only provide jobs to top competitive video gamers. The esports industry can be compared to football or baseball in the way that each league provides thousands of well-paying non-athlete jobs. The esports industry has now grown to include everything you can expect from traditional sports and more.

11 CAREERS IN ESPORTS

To learn more about careers in esports, I had the chance to interview Emil Bodenstein after he spoke at the 2019 StreamGeeks Summit on the Esports Panel. Emil is a former computer science teacher who is now the CEO of an esports agency called Alpha North Esports. Bodenstein has transitioned from a career as a professional athlete agent to a career leading a company in the esports industry. Bodenstein first got involved with esports when the professional baseball athletes that he represented asked him if they could start their own gaming competition. Always up to a challenge, Bodenstein ended up working with the Major League Baseball Players Association to organize a celebrity only gaming league that was very successful. Around the same time, Bodenstein recalls hearing about the 2016 League of Legends tournament that was able to sell out the Madison Square Garden in just 24 hours. Putting two and two together, Bodenstein started to make plans to look for a career in the growing esports industry.

"Unlike traditional sports such as baseball and football, where the audience primarily comes from America. With esports, the audience is global. These games are being translated and streamed in different languages all around the world. The growth rate is unprecedented" says Bodenstein. The good news is that Bodenstein is optimistic about the esports job market. "One of the studies we looked at showed that major league franchises have on average over 200 non-athlete jobs. We compared this data to esports franchises and found that they currently only have around 10 non-athlete jobs. This means there is a ton of room for growth." Coming from the world of professional sports, Bodenstein has a unique perspective on how major league sports franchises currently operate. "If you want your team to win, you have to hire scouts who can go out and watch games in order to find talent. In baseball, you have national cross checkers, regional cross checkers, area scouts, and even international scouts. Because these esports franchises are competing worldwide, talent scouting will become a major job in esports." Other jobs include data analytics, health and wellness, coaching, training, content creation, and marketing. "Health and wellness industries are already a growing area of esports. In football, for example, you are constantly testing your flexibility and strength. Esports will eventually need to test areas such as reaction times and communication capabilities. This could include neurological testing. Esports games are mainly played sitting down. Athletes will require massage therapy, and chiropractors to stay in shape and maintain peak performance. Entire industries are adapting their business models to include the esports industry in some way."

While many new jobs will be created by the esports industry, Bodenstein explained some of the issues with an industry that is growing at such astronomical rates. With the industry's most popular games changing so frequently, publishers hold incredible control over the tournaments. With esports, game publishers essentially own the "Baseball" or "Football" game that is popular at any given time. When a publisher like Epic Games, for example, creates the world's most popular video game, they have to scale at unprecedented rates to manage their worldwide tournaments. Epic Games, for example, had no sponsors involved in their latest Fortnite World Cup. "Imagine having the World Series with no sponsors," says Bodenstein. "Game developers like Blizzard are following the sports model, with franchises and commissioners by creating leagues for their games. But Fortnite has not yet created a formal franchise model. Epic games currently control everything involving their tournaments. It's unprecedented in the world of sports" says Bodenstein.

ESPORTS MONTHLY AUDIENCE SIZE TODAY VS. WHERE IT'S HEADING (Source Goldman Sachs)

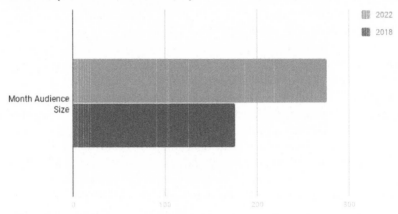

A new report from Goldman Sachs shared their estimates on the growth of revenue generated by esports. In 2017, media rights represented only 14% of all revenue. In 2022, Goldman Sachs predicts media rights will be 40% of all revenue. This type of growth means game publishers and sponsors will need to hire marketing and advertising firms to manage the process. A landmark deal mentioned in the report is a two-year media rights deal between Activision and Twitch. The $90 million dollar deal gives Twitch the rights to broadcast the Overwatch league in North America. The report projects global esports audiences to grow from 167 million in 2018 to 276 million in 2022. The report says "The audiences on YouTube and Twitch are larger than HBO, Netflix, and ESPN combine" (Goldman Sachs, 2019).

Esports Revenue Streams 2017

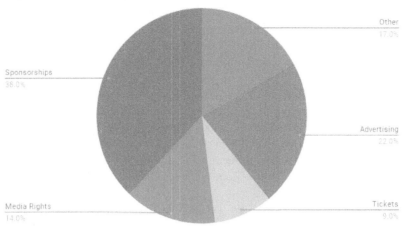

Other
17.0%

Sponsorships
38.0%

Advertising
22.0%

Media Rights
14.0%

Tickets
9.0%

Esports Revenue Streams 2022

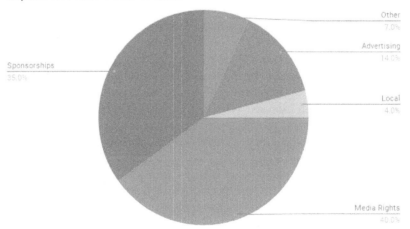

Other
7.0%

Advertising
14.0%

Sponsorships
35.0%

Local
4.0%

Media Rights
40.0%

Jobs in marketing are another booming position in this new esports job market. National brands on the consumer side are rapidly getting involved with esports. Brands are hiring new marketing positions to manage their relationships and seek out new partnerships in the esports industry. Brands like Nike, for example, now offer digital versions of their shoes which Fortnite gamers can wear. The opportunity for businesses and video game developers to work together looks very promising.

With all the great jobs available today, I asked Bodenstein if he had any advice for students who are aspiring to become professional esports athletes. "You have to have a plan b… I don't tell my kids that they can't get a job in esports, but it's important to be realistic. When you are playing the top video games in the world you must understand the challenges that you are up against. Most students can compete at a high school level. That should be your goal and allow your abilities to take it from there. Your back up plan should be first and foremost your education. So that you can get a job once you leave school… Remember, Ninja started out as a Halo player. He took a chance with a new game called Fortnite. Don't just stick to the games that are super popular. Some of the newer games may take off and it could benefit you to try new things. Most games don't have a very long shelf life. How long is Fortnite going to stay on top?"

With such great job opportunities available in esports today, here are a few tips to prepare for success in finding a full-time job after school. Building your resume to succeed in esports can be done by gaining experience in esports related activities. An easy way to get involved is to volunteer at a local esports tournament. A few easy ways to participate include helping as a community manager, event organizer, content creator, journalist, tournament admin, referee, coach or shoutcaster (aka announcer). Adding real-world experience to your resume in any of these positions will show potential employers you are involved with the industry. As you build your resume with real-world experiences, consider starting an online blog. Start a gaming blog that you can use to outline your experiences in detail. Writing is a valuable educational tool that can help you internalize learning from experiences like video gaming or volunteering. Consider joining your school's esports club and getting involved to stay up to date with upcoming esports opportunities. Did you know that creating your own video game may not be as hard as you think? Look into the latest tools for creating a video game and see if some of your friends at school want to help. Once your game is complete, add it to your resume as well. If you really like video games, a fun entry-level job you can apply for is a video game tester. As you explore opportunities in esports, consider if you want to take your education to the next level and apply to colleges with esports and video game-related programs. With a modern college degree and a resume full of esports specific experience, you are setting yourself up for success in the esports industry.

Millennials (those born between 1981 and 1996) are now the largest generation in the workforce. Research shows millennials change jobs more than other generations and the turnover actually costs the U.S economy $30.5 billion per year. More than generations in the past, millennials want to "work for themselves" and they prefer freedom over high paying salaries. It's no surprise that millennials like to have the "latest and greatest" technologies and this trend sets them apart in the workplace. Millennials are the most studied generation in history and the research clearly shows they are more willing to try new things and switch careers. With new emerging jobs and opportunities online, millennials are a generation willing to try to make career moves that might seem riskier to non-digital natives. This is one reason why companies like Twitch who offer millennials the ability to make money playing video games online have been so popular. One company called StreamLabs that helps Twitch streamer monetize their online game streams was recently sold in 2019 for $89 million dollars. Twitch recently reported that they have 2.2 million daily broadcasters with over 15 million daily viewers. These numbers make cable television look small, and their success is in part due to the real careers they are helping to create for millennials (Emmons, n.d).

12 ESPORTS AND TRADITIONAL SPORTS COLLIDE

Some of the most popular competitive video games are based on established sports such as the NFL, MLB, NBA, and FIFA. The company EA Sports, which is a division of Electronic Arts, spends billions in royalty contracts with official sports networks to develop its popular line of video games. These video games are made specifically to imitate real-life sports and allow players the ability to play as their favorite professional athletes. Jadd Schmeltzer, the Esports Director at the Center for Educational Innovation (CEI), is working with students throughout the New York City area using sports-based video games as a way to excite student learning in innovative ways.

The Center for Educational Innovation supports traditional public schools and public charter schools with student-centered innovations, customized support, and life-changing enrichment programs for at-risk students. The organization works directly with school leaders, teachers, students, and the community to create high performing schools in low-resourced areas. As the Esports Director for CEI, Schmeltzer has developed a program that focuses on "Experiential Learning Opportunities" through competitive esports. Schmeltzer is an early innovator in the world of esports and education during a time when the NCAA (National Collegiate Athletic Association) has voted to table the possibility of overseeing and holding college-level championships for esports. It's an interesting moment in history where many major colleges and universities want to prepare students the way that Schmeltzer can with his program yet established governing authorities like the NCAA see esports as a threat to their organization. Deborah M. Grzybowski, the co-director of game studies and esports curriculum at Ohio State says "Companies have noted to various people on campus that we're not putting out students with all the skills that they need to fill the job openings they have in the esports area." Despite the NCAA's announcements to restrict esports from becoming a varsity-level sport associated with most school athletics departments, schools like Ohio State, the University of Utah and many others have found ways to create programs outside of the NCAA's reach. Esports culture challenges the NCAA's bylaws which restrict student-athletes from being monetarily compensated. Most esports players who are good enough to receive a scholarship already have multiple sources of revenue that they generate from their capabilities (Smith, 2018).

Unlike many college-level athletic departments' that partner with the NCAA, Schmeltzer can innovate under the CEI's mission to create life-changing enrichment programs. He has built an educational curriculum that provides students with "touchpoints" for real-world career opportunities in the esports industry. Where Smeltzer's program really gets interesting is his use of NBA2K, a basketball video game developed by Take-Two Interactive. NBA2K has its own "NBA2K League" with real-world tournaments and prizes, just like League of Legends and DOTA2. Scheltmzer told me that, "70% of students stop playing sports after the age of 13" and his program uses video games like NBA2K to teach sports in new engaging ways to further student exposure to sports. When you think about the fact that 90% of teens are playing video games every day, Schmeltzer's approach starts to make a lot of sense.

Teaching basketball through the power of video games allows students to experience the thrill of professional-level gameplay. From an educational perspective, Schmeltzer is able to work with students who can use the experience to better understand the underlying strategies and value of teamwork. Throughout the educational process, the program's curriculum includes touchpoints in many career categories including business, design, journalism, marketing, and more. These touchpoints provide students with real-world experiences that can help influence their decisions about what careers they may be interested in.

"Students are excited about working in the esports industry," says Schmeltzer. This program helps students set realistic goals about entering the esports job market from a career perspective. While tournament prizes and scholarships for esports are great tools for motivation, Schmeltzer's program helps to prepare students for roles in the esports industry that draws on real-world career paths.

It's interesting to note that many esports teams are dedicated to learning a single game, such as Fortnite, League of Legends, or Defense of the Ancients 2. A known issue in esports team organizations is how quickly games can change and players can be left with skills that are no longer applicable. With such short time periods for players to compete professionally, it can seem impossible for athletes to switch games mid-career. Schmeltzer foresees a major focus on esports games that represent real traditional sports networks for this reason. Traditional sports like the NBA are world-wide brands that continue to grow internationally. With esports programs that are based on professional sports like the NBA there is little worry that the game will no longer be popular in 2025. The program is also able to bring students to real professional basketball games and take their mission to further experiential learning to the next level.

At the 2019 StreamGeeks Summit, Schmeltzer was able to team up with the S.A.R High School to introduce students to the video production side of esports. This esports tournament is a great example where a student-run video production team had the chance to experience many career roles, which include journalism, on-camera work, video production, camera operation and more. Helping students gain volunteer opportunities within esports tournaments is a great way for students to build esports related experiences for their resumes.

13 AN INSIDER VIEW INTO ESPORTS

During the 2019 NAB (National Association of Broadcasters) Show, I hosted a panel on esports with three industry professionals who are doing great things in esports. The panel included Tim Vandenburg of vMix, Stu Grubbs of LightStream, and Norris Howard from CheckPointXP. Along with my co-host, Tess Protesto, I had a chance to chat with these gentlemen about various aspects of the industry. This group of panelists has been in esports long enough to know the unique challenges players face and what the future holds for the sport. Here is a summary of the salient points in the interview.

What is the age-range, generally, for the top esports competitors?

Grubbs: Typically, eighteen to twenty-five.

Howard: After twenty-five, you don't have many players able to stay competitive.

Grubbs: Younger than eighteen and you don't have the maturity to play as a team and understand the strategy of the game. Over twenty-five and you start to lose the mental agility. Because those athletes who play at the highest levels, they will whip their mouse in a fraction of a second and get that headshot.

Vandenburg: Yeah, you watch some of these ex-professionals, like "Ninja" and it is amazing to see how good they are; but then you watch the guys at the tournaments and those guys are even better.

Howard: Yeah, because they are doing all of that on a high-stage and in high-pressure situations.

Grubbs: To give you an idea, when Starcraft II was the big popular game in esports, a lot of Koreans dominated that scene. They were performing two to three hundred actions per minute to be considered a professional player. Actions being key-presses, mouse-clicks, and movements. They had to do that while managing, maybe, three economies and seeing only a glimpse of their opponent's base and understanding what units they needed to build to counter that.

Do you guys think the ability to become professional in Esports is on par compared to other professional sports?

Howard: Definitely easier than traditional sports because there is no physical barrier; for instance, you could be the greatest jumper in the world, but if you're 4 ft 11" you are not going to get into the NBA. If you have a stable internet connection and you have dedication, there is a real avenue for going pro in esports, no matter what your build is like.

Grubbs: There are no statutory limitations, but from the training side, people who are finding success in esports make a tremendous amount of effort to be better at the game, to the point where it sort of becomes a full-time job. Most avid professional esports players have a physical regimen they go through and there is also a level of intelligence required in most of the games.

Vandenburg: Right now, accessibility is high and anyone with a PC or mobile phone can get into games. Getting to a professional level is another thing entirely. There is a physical element to it, not necessarily athletic abilities, but you need hand-eye coordination, along with the ability to perform high numbers of clicks-per-minute and so forth. Additionally, there are lots of games out there and what you need to become good is different for each one.

There is so much growth in the industry. There are the Twitch-streamers, the tournaments, and the official teams with big name brands. What do you think is having the most impact on the industry?

Grubbs: I would say nothing has had a bigger impact on esports' growth than live streaming. The proliferation of content around competitive play when competitors are not at tournaments, being able to view them on a personal streaming channel, getting to know them and their play style better, and then seeing them compete in a tournament. There is a constant touchpoint for fans and they are continually involved, instead of just seeing the tournaments every three months, as it was back before live streaming. Back then, when we first started, our big goal was, "let's get on TV; once we get esports on TV, we will be accepted." The reality right now is that nobody cares about TV because everyone is consuming content through live streaming.

Howard: I would second that. Twitch has been transformative for competitive gaming. Without it, it was rough to consistently get any real content and consume it from a realistic standpoint. With that also comes the infrastructure that has been put into esports, especially in the last five years. By putting more infrastructure into it, we now have something like the Overwatch League, which is like the gold standard for presentation, infrastructure, and sales of esports.

I imagine streaming has opened up a lot of opportunities for gamers that have a lot of talent to get recognized, right?

Vandenburg: Not necessarily. A lot of the Twitch streamers, many of them are ex-professional guys. They are launching their careers after esports, sort of. That is because their careers are not that long because you lose the ability to be as fast as you used to be.

Grubbs: That is correct; that is why Tyler "Ninja" Blevins is no longer a competitor, but then he suddenly blows up and becomes one of the most popular streamers in the world.

If live-streaming is the biggest thing in esports and Twitch is right in the middle of it, tell us about TwitchCon. What was it like to be there? I understand there were lines going around the building, like two or three times around.

Vandenburg: It is crazy, especially if you are coming from the outside. It was definitely an experience, but it was not just about esports. It was about all the different areas of streaming. They were doing things on the artwork, music, creating costumes, and jewelry, plus the esports side of things. Twitch is a massive place right now and the conference was such an overwhelming experience to see.

Grubbs: You also had a part of the show that covered broadcast tools, hardware, chairs, lighting, and even esports drinks. For example, energy drinks to keep you up when you are gaming. Then, the games themselves were all set up. There were games built with streaming in mind; how to engage your audience in the game. So TwitchCon was about every aspect of the gaming industry.

We are from Philadelphia and we were shocked to learn that we have a huge esports arena being built in our city. Is this where the industry is headed? Is it the individual streamer, the tournaments or the teams that are driving this industry?

Howard: I think it is both. There is room enough for people who are very skilled, but may not want to participate in the bigger scene. However, it also benefits cities and organizations to build these arenas and bring those big events to their local economies. The investment and excitement is there right now and if they do not jump on it now, they may get left behind.

Grubbs: I am not sold on arenas yet. I like the idea; they worked really well in Korea. I have even seen a few of them. In some cases they have done really well, but in others they have not gathered the kind of audience they thought they would. This is partly because these teams are franchises and the sports will constantly switch to whatever is the hottest game right now. What would be interesting to see is how teams switch players into the games that are currently the most popular.

Vandenburg: Yes, because if you look at teams right now, they are not spread across different games. Each team is specific to the games they play. The arenas are adding more legitimacy and that is what people want. However, has it gone too big, too quick? It is really an interesting time and we just have to wait to see what happens.

14 STARTING AN ESPORTS CLUB AT YOUR

SCHOOL

You may be thinking to yourself, "Hey, I'm a good candidate for helping my school start an esports club." Many school districts do not yet have esports set up as an official sport and therefore, creating a club may be the best place to start. Until competitive esports become an official sport at your school, you can take the following basic steps to start organizing a school-sponsored club. Esports clubs can cover many aspects of esports and student involvement. If your school does decide to start a varsity level esports program, you may be surprised that the esports club maintains its importance as a partner organization with the athletics department.

Find a teacher or faculty member mentor

Finding an adult at your school who is willing to help lead the esports club is an ideal first step. A great club sponsor could be a teacher involved in the AV department, the broadcast club, the robotics club, or other technology-related roles. It's best to find a member of the school's faculty or staff who has experience with school clubs. Even if your club sponsor does not have a personal interest in video games, it's helpful if they understand how clubs are established at your unique school. Obviously, finding someone with experience playing video games is a plus. Try downloading the free PDF version of this book and asking the faculty member to read it. (Available at ptzoptics.com/book).

Get the word out

It's important to get the word out about your idea when you are trying to start a new esports club. Find out who may be interested in helping you get started. You can start with teachers and then move on to the student council. You may be surprised how quickly the word will spread when you have a good idea. To help in the process, the online course for Esports in Education includes a flyer template you can use. Consider creating some digital files that you can share. You can use the images to email to friends, post on Facebook, and print out for flyers. The online course materials also include a customizable email signature that you can use. Does your school have a Facebook Group? You can also try using a local neighborhood network such as Nextdoor to get the word out.

Word of mouth is perhaps the most powerful tool at your disposal. So it's important to explain clearly what you are trying to do. It's always helpful to write down the reason why your school should start an esports club. Keep a running list of students, parents and teachers who are interested in helping your cause. You can create an online form that people can fill out with their information to organize your supporter list.

Write it down on Paper

Start an "Esports Club Creation Document" that you can share with other students and teachers about your new esports club. Don't worry about getting every detail perfect in this document. Let everyone know that you are in the process of figuring out all the details. Have a list of questions you are trying to get answered and remember it's okay if you don't have all of the answers. Start by doing some research online. See if your school is in an area with a high school esports league. If there is a league that is in your local area, you can start to gather information about what it takes to join. These local leagues often have resources you can leverage to get started.

Work with other students to create a document that outlines the following details:

1. Who is the club sponsor?
2. When will the club meet?
3. Where will the club meet?

4. What are the club goals?
    a. What are the short-term goals?
    b. What are the long-term goals?
5. Is there an Esports League you will join?
6. Does the league have seasons?
7. Are there other schools in your area you can model your club after?
8. Are there local competitions you should note?
9. How many players are needed on your roster?
10. Are there age requirements?
11. Are there any academic eligibility requirements?
12. Does the league require a coach?
13. What equipment will be required for gameplay?

Once you have organized the information above, you should be able to give your school a good idea of what you are trying to accomplish.

Recruit Your Team

Share your club explanation document with friends who are interested in joining. It will be important for each student to share the document with their parents. The document should include times and locations for team practices and official league tournaments. If you have chosen an esports league in your area, be sure to share that information with everyone. Most leagues have an online platform that can enable your club to easily build and manage your team. Each player will get a log in so that students, teachers, and parents can all check schedules, track stats and follow along with the official league.

Most leagues will charge a per player fee. There are usually two competitive seasons and there may also be pre and post seasons. PlayVs, for example, has a preseason that starts in October and a "Regular Season" that runs from late October into December. Share all of this information to help recruit your team. Everyone should know the commitments required for joining the club.

Organizing Your Team

You can start by determining which game your team will focus on. Popular games supported by most leagues include League of Legends, Rocket League, and Smite. The game that you choose will become a central focus for your team. You should choose a game that you understand, and your entire team can all agree on. The game selection process is important, and your team's coach should be involved. You can start by selecting multiple possible games that the league you are interested in joining supports. Compare and contrast the differences between each game carefully.

Once you have selected the game your team will train and compete for, it's time to start researching the game. Your coach should have an in-depth understanding of the game, which they can use to guide the team. If your club does not have a coach, your club leader may have to take on a leadership role as "interim coach." During your research, you will uncover strategies that will require communication and teamwork. Your team should always communicate and discuss strategy before starting a practice session.

During club meetings, start an agenda that can be used to discuss the club's goals and progress that is being made toward those goals. If your club has access to a shared folder, such as Google Drive or Dropbox folder, you can organize your meeting notes there. Stay organized and create folders for each season, which can contain the notes from each meeting.

Review the below example agenda and feel free to customize it for your team.

Esports Club Meeting Agenda

Objectives			
Topic	Time	Suggested Reflection or Exercises	Notes:
Greeting	5 Min	Briefly review last meeting's notes Check up on the progress of on-going club goals Review at-home research	
Planning / Training Regimen	10 Min	What is the goal for today? What is the current training regimen?	
Coaching	10 Min	Coach Review Notes	
Practice	30 Min	Practice Gaming	
Closing	5 Min	At Home Research/Efforts	

Team Branding

Creating a brand for your new esports team will help spread the word and build team pride. Think about creating a catchy name that represents your school, the area you are from, or the interests of your team. You should have a club meeting to talk through all the various aspects of branding your team. You will need to come up with a team name, colors, and a logo. You can outsource the creation of a logo to someone in your school who is talented with digital design. Alternatively, you can find a freelancer on a website such as Fiverr. Once you have the basics of your team branding done, it's time to create a website.

Having a website is a crucial step to building your team's fanbase. Consider taking pictures of everyone on your team and including social media handles for each player. You can use your "Esports Club Creation Document" to share with the world all the pertinent information about your team. Keep your website clean and professional. You can include a "contact us" form on your website or share an email address. You may be surprised when a local newspaper or video game company asks to interview your team. Once your website is complete see if the school has a place to post a link to your website. You can go online and register your club's website in many online directories to help people find it. Your website can also include a blog that can be used to update the world on your journey. Writing about your training regimen, gameplay, and meeting notes is a great exercise to further the learning of your entire club.

Team Building

When you are first starting an esports club, do not worry about recruiting the best players in the world. Esports clubs should be a safe place for students who are interested in competitive video gaming to get their start. With that being said, it is normal to hold "tryouts" for positions on the starting team. Your club's faculty sponsor should be able to help hold tryouts and create a team that consists of not just the "best" players but also the most dedicated. Remember that to create a dynamic esports team, you will want players who share your passion for success. Your coach should be able to prepare students for the ups and downs of competitive video gameplay. Speak with your club sponsor about the maximum club size that they feel comfortable supporting. Normally groups over 30 people can become unproductive due to size. If your club grows beyond 30 members you should consider adding an additional coach or adult faculty member.

Your school may already have guidelines in place to handle large school clubs. During tryouts don't forget to be inclusive. Just because someone is not on the "starting team" doesn't mean that they won't have other valuable skills. Learning how to work as a team and overall organization is one of the greatest lessons that school clubs can offer students.

Equipment Setup

Just like any sport, there are some required items each player will need access to. At a minimum, for competitive esports gameplay, each player will require a computer, keyboard, and mouse connected to a LAN (Local Area Network) of some sort. While prices for gaming equipment continue to come down each year, if your team needs multiple gaming computers, this could become costly. Cloud-based gaming is now lowering the price points for esports clubs to get started (more on this soon).

It may be most practical for the club to host practices at a local gaming center. Gaming centers will often have discounts for teams that practice at their facilities. If your team uses a local gaming center for practices, then the facilities at school can be used for club meetings that focus on organization and strategy. If your school has a space where equipment can be set up, your team can consider fundraising. This is a great way to spread awareness and gather the money your team needs to purchase esports equipment. There may be grants available to your school for esports, so consider searching around for available sources of funding. The StreamGeeks offer an annual $1,000 Esports Scholarship you can apply for at streamgeeks.us/esports. If your team decides to start fundraising, you will need to determine your exact goal. Create a list of all the equipment your team needs to practice in a given space.

Even if you must practice at a gaming center for multiple seasons, your team can still represent your school and compete in tournaments. You may consider speaking with the school technology department faculty. Consider inquiring about the use of school computer labs and areas with dedicated computers in place. You may be surprised how supportive your school's technology faculty are to your cause.

Online Tools

Today's tech-savvy esports clubs are always using the latest online tools to communicate and stay organized. Perhaps the most central online tool for esports clubs use is a Discord server. Discord is a freeware software application that is designed specifically for video game communities. Starting a Discord server is incredibly easy, and once you have set it up the service can become the hub for your team's online communications. Your Discord server can be set up to use specific channels to organize topics for your club.

For example, you may want to start with the following channels:

- Club Meeting Notes
- Upcoming Tournaments
- Practice Notes
- Strategy Notes
- Training Regimen
- Casual, Humor, Interest

Everyone on your team should be invited to your Discord server via email. Your server will be available from any web browser or via a free client software that can run on any Mac, PC, or Linux computer. Members of your team should be encouraged to keep their conversations relevant to the channel they are using. If they are just joking around, it should be done in the "Casual, Humor, Interest" channel. If you have a question regarding the club's schedule that should be posted in "Upcoming Tournaments." In this way, you can quickly access and organize the information your club needs by selecting the channel it should be inside.

Another great online tool for online communications is called TeamSpeak. This is a cloud-based voice-over IP application that allows teams of esports players to communicate. Discord does offer a very similar voice communications system, which is completely free. However, TeamSpeak offers better quality for a minimal price. Whether you are using Discord or TeamSpeak, everyone on your team will need a USB headset to communicate. Using communication tools like this will allow your team to practice from home or anywhere in the world.

Training

When your team meets each week, you should always be talking about your training regimen. It's important to have everyone on your team to discuss the specific skills that they want to work on. Allowing everyone on your team a moment to reflect on these skills will also help increase team communications. Your team coach should be involved in creating and maintaining the training regimen. As the training regimen evolves an online document can be maintained and posted in your Discord channel for "Training Regimen."

A good training program should be customized for each player. Coaches should always include a team skill-building section, along with a personalized skill-building section for each player. Personalized skill-building can be game-specific or gaming-specific. Game-specific training can include increasing players' overall knowledge of how the game works and the strategy behind competitive gameplay. Game-specific research can involve watching others play the game and taking notes that can be shared with the club. Gaming-specific skill development covers a wider variety of skills that could apply to any game, such as training for hand-eye coordination, team communication skills, and critical thinking.

Team training exercises should be explored both online and off. Online, your team should learn about each player's unique gameplay styles and areas of skill. Teams who learn how to play together win together. Coaches should help teams develop their communication skills and identify various players for crucial roles in the team. Offline teams can work on teamwork principles such as trust, friendship, and communication. Take the time to consider the game you have selected, the players on your team, and the roles that you need to fill.

Cloud-Based Gaming

As of early 2020, cloud-based gaming has set a new course for the world of video gaming. Microsoft xCloud, PlayStation Now and Google Stadia are all leaders in the cloud gaming space. Cloud gaming is very similar to on-demand video streaming services such as Netflix and Hulu. These services allow customers to subscribe for a low monthly fee and gain access to an ever-changing and up to date catalog of content. Cloud-based gaming will offer the same type of low-cost access to video games. PlayStation Now, for example, costs just $9.99 per month and offers customers access to over 800 games that they can play on their PC or PlayStation consoles. Microsoft's Project xCloud is still in beta but it promises users a similar solution. Project xCloud allows players to connect a Bluetooth Xbox controller to any smartphone or tablet to allow users to play Xbox games. This idea is revolutionary because gamers can now use mobile phones they already have and skip purchasing expensive gaming consoles. Google's Stadia platform takes affordability and convenience even further with a platform that allows players to use a Google Chromecast connected to any TV. Stadia also supports almost any tablet, smartphone, or computer.

What does cloud gaming mean for the future of esports? There are well-known issues with cloud-based gaming that will prevent high stakes esports tournaments from using the cloud. The main issue with cloud gaming is latency. Latency is also known as "lag" and it is not tolerated in esports tournaments. The latency between players can create an inconsistent playing experience that is inferior to the traditional computer or console systems connected to a local area network. A local area network does not require internet access to servers located around the world over the public internet. While the cloud offers many benefits, using the public internet is the main culprit creating latency. While cloud gaming isn't going to replace consoles for competitive gameplay, it will change the gaming landscape in many important ways.

Cloud gaming is going to allow millions of new gamers to access high-quality gaming experiences at incredibly low costs. It's possible that esports clubs can now set up practice spaces without the need for purchasing expensive video gaming gear. Cloud-based gaming is also incredibly easy to set up reducing technical barriers to entry for the everyday teacher or student who wants to set up a small gaming area. Google chrome books, for example, can be purchased for under $200 each. In most developed countries, most teenagers already have smartphones that can now be used to play esports in school clubs. This is a big difference between the costs of dedicated gaming machines which can easily cost more than $1,000 or $2,000. This type of massive change will bring millions of new players online in developed and developing countries around the world.

Other benefits of cloud-based gaming include instant access to new games without the hassle of downloads and updates. Does anyone remember keeping an old collection of DVDs at home? How about downloading music or videos and organizing all of those files on a local hard drive? Nobody does that anymore. Today streaming services have replaced the need for local media storage and put the power of streaming media in the hands of anyone with an internet-connected device. The same is true with cloud gaming and Google says "There's no need to overpay for expensive hardware. With Stadia, you get up to 4K 60 FPS gameplay on TVs without the hassle of time-consuming game downloads or in-game updates. And you can take your favorite games with you on your laptop, tablet, or phone as long as you have Wi-Fi." Just imagine all the kids you see in restaurants sitting with their parents watching YouTube on smartphones. Now imagine these smartphones have access to high-end video gaming servers. It's now totally possible for competitive video games to be played anywhere in the world with an internet connection.

When it comes to new esports clubs, many are just getting started with little to no budget. Faced with low budget constraints most students understand that "Good Enough" is a perfect starting point. If esports clubs can get their start with a subscription to a cloud gaming service and the use of an old smartphone, the democratization of competitive video gaming will truly begin. Students can now use a smartphone or low powered computer to practice their skills from anywhere with a decent internet connection (10Mbps download speeds are generally recommended). Competitive video gaming in the cloud will be very much like the lower pressure scrimmage games popular in other sports. Professional gaming consoles and networking equipment will still be required for high stakes competitive gaming. But the new doors that are now opening for young aspiring esports athletes will change the global gaming landscape forever.

15 SIDE BY SIDE BROADCAST CLUBS AND ESPORTS

Through the process of writing a book called the *Accelerated Broadcast Club Curriculum*, I had the opportunity to meet with student-run broadcast clubs from around the world. After learning so much about what's going on in esports, it was clear to me that broadcast clubs and esports programs have a lot in common. One school, the S.A.R High School in the New York City area, impressed me with their innovative way of live streaming school sports. When a particularly talented broadcast club member, Ian Fuller, had the chance to live stream an esports tournament it became clear that the skills he acquired from the broadcasting club could be transferred over to esports production.

Through a strong interest in broadcasting sports, the S.A.R High School Broadcast Club has become the biggest club at the school. One of the most popular student positions is the "Play-by-Play" announcer. Whether you are broadcasting a football game or a RocketLeague tournament, students and spectators love to hear good sports commentary during gameplay. Commentators or "Shoutcasters" as they are called in esports, are great on or off-camera roles for students who want to get involved with the broadcast club or esports.

Many broadcast clubs have found that broadcasting school sports can become popular for both students and family members at home. Online video has changed the world in so many ways, students are often the first to understand how powerful the medium can be. Families who are unable to attend school events are usually the first to comment about how important the online video is.

Here is a list of non-athlete roles/careers students can be involved with esports and broadcast clubs:

1. Event Planning
2. Web Development
3. Health and Wellness
4. Athletic Coaching
5. Video Production
6. Journalism
7. Entrepreneurship

8.   Marketing
9.   Digital Media
10.   Broadcasting
11.   Social Media

If you think about it, esports programs have more in common with school broadcast clubs than most other clubs in schools today. Broadcast clubs that are currently helping their school sports teams are often thanked for assisting the athletic departments. Some students are even able to increase their chances of securing scholarships by providing video footage to college scouts via email. In the same vein, esports students who are helped by the broadcast club to live stream tournaments can use the video footage as well. There are now many scholarships available to students who excel in competitive esports.

Josh Lewis, the faculty sponsor, and broadcast club manager says, "We are a Google Apps for Education school and every student has their own school email address from us. The club can use Google Apps to give students access to shared documents." Lewis explained to me that the club uses Google Sites to help students get involved with the clubs' website development. Web development is an interesting aspect of esports programs that students can help contribute to. "After a couple of years of archiving all of our videos on YouTube… We found that there were also a lot of pictures and the school didn't have an official athletics website. So, we sort of melded the broadcasting and athletics website with team rosters, videos, and game setlists all in one place… Google Sites is free and it's on our school domain. Google Sites are just like a Google Doc where I can share control of certain portions of the site for students to interact with an update." Similarly, esports programs have the need to organize team rosters and activities online.

The website includes a convenient integration with Google Calendars. Since the school already leverages Google Calendars to organize school events, it was easy to integrate this shared calendar with the website. Public Google Calendars can have an HTML embed code generated and published on a website for public viewing. In this way, the information is organized by the team's coaches, faculty, and staff members. As schools start to develop their esports programs, leveraging the tools they already have access to, like the Google Suite for Education, will make collaborations like this more practical.

By using Google Calendars in this way, the broadcast club's website always reflects the latest information about school sports with minimal burden on the group. This type of frictionless integration between scheduling applications and a public website makes life easy for students, parents, and faculty members. Multiple sports team schedules including basketball, wrestling, hockey, volleyball and more are all integrated into one sortable calendar interface.

Lewis also explained to me how the club uses Google Sheets to organize volunteer roles for camera operators, live stream operators, and announcers. The club starts out choosing a list of sports games that they will live stream each semester. Lewis will generally consult with team coaches about choosing a game or two that they are particularly interested in having recorded via video. Once the list is compiled, the students involved with the club will have access to only the Google Sheet columns that allow them to volunteer for a specific role. This is a modern way to keep students involved in the club and collect volunteer information. Organizing esports tournaments with multiple rounds of qualifications can be managed with Google Sheets as well.

After about one year of broadcasting the school's sports teams, Lewis started getting calls from coaches asking where they could find the recorded video. Lewis estimated that for every five people watching a school sports game live, there are perhaps 100 people who watch the video replay on-demand. "Even if we only have five or ten people watching live, our videos will generally have a couple of hundred views the next day on YouTube," says Lewis. This is, of course, because not everyone can watch the broadcast clubs' content while it's live. Many of the student-athletes study the video after the broadcast to improve upon their skills. The same is true for recorded and live-streamed esports gameplay. Good esports coaches can review footage with players to discuss strategy in a similar fashion.

Lewis told me that, "the students are watching the video after it has been streamed and the coaches are watching as well. They are breaking down parts of the game and trying to determine where they could have done better... Certain coaches will email the students a link to the live stream and ask them to watch the live stream again and breakdown certain players on the opposing team... We live stream a game and then later in the season, we play that same team again. There are certain sports such as volleyball, where you can really gain a competitive advantage, looking at certain players. For example, one player may only serve short or they only serve long."

The same type of competitive analysis and training is happening within the next generation of esports clubs. It's valuable to look at what broadcast clubs are doing today with established sports in order to foresee a future where esports are taken just as seriously as baseball and football in school athletics. Most esports teams can easily find and study recorded video footage available of opponents they will be playing in upcoming tournaments.

It's quite common for the club to get requests from coaches and teachers for what the club calls "highlight reels." Coaches especially will send the club requests for specific time stamps inside live streams, which the club will edit down into a more digestible format. The club likes to use iMovie for simple video editing and they currently leverage Final Cut Pro for more advanced projects. "The first thing we usually do is download our live stream from YouTube." says Lewis. If the video was recorded directly to an SD card, this footage will likely be of a higher quality than our YouTube recording that was live-streamed. We can download our YouTube video by going into the creator studio in YouTube and by clicking the icon logo in the top right corner of YouTube, then clicking *Creator Studio*. Inside Creator Studio we can select the *Video Manager* and find the video you would like to download for editing. We can click the drop-down menu and select *Download MP4*" says Lewis.

This story from the S.A.R High School demonstrates just how integral this broadcast club has become inside the school's athletics department. Most schools today already have digital media and broadcast clubs in place, which can help newly started esports programs prosper. You can see that student roles in broadcasting, team management, digital media, photography, and web development are all encouraged throughout the process. In the next chapter, you will learn about a student-run broadcast that operates the morning announcements at the Griswold High School. This type of student-run production can be easily adapted to the "Play-by-Play" esports broadcaster roles now popular in esports tournaments. After interviewing many high school broadcast clubs, the Griswold High School stood out as an innovator in more ways than one.

16 MORNING ANNOUNCEMENTS AND ESPORTS SHOUTCASTERS

It's no surprise that student retention rates skyrocket when it comes to hands-on learning. Hands-on learning increases our engagement because it provides the opportunity to interact with the subject matter in a way that feels real. When it comes to understanding broadcast television and streaming media, there is no better way to learn. Walking into a student-run production room during the morning announcements is a sight to see. It may sound cliché, but practice does make perfect and the students at Griswold High School in Griswold, Connecticut get 180 days of practice every year. As an added bonus, the entire school gets updated on important school news, sports, the weather, and birthdays.

Student Retention Rates

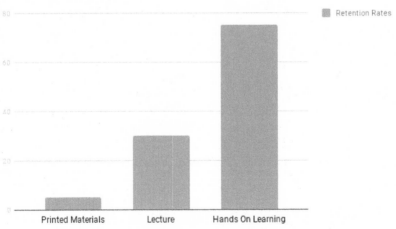

I first met the 2018 class of the Griswold High School's student-run broadcast club on the 2018 Streaming Awards show. The Streaming Awards are an annual event hosted by the StreamGeeks, where we acknowledge live streaming shows from around the world. This awards show happens every year and the voting is 100% audience-driven. With hundreds of contestants from all around the world, some members of our audience were surprised that a high school news announcement team was hovering around the number one and number two ranks for the popular vote.

Teacher Timothy Moore started the Griswold School Broadcast Club in 1991 and this year, the club had 16 student members from grades nine through twelve. The Griswold Broadcast Club reflects the organizational structure of a traditional television production studio, which includes a producer, director, technical director, audio chief, teleprompter chiefs, character generators, and on-screen talent. An organizational structure like this allows students to come into the program as a freshman and rise through the ranks each year. Esports programs should consider roles that students can progress through to encourage growth through the program. Requirements to join the club can also include a minimum GPA to encourage a focus on academics.

Moore takes on the producer role himself during each student announcements production. "It is a student-run organization, I am just here to sit back and watch things go smoothly… and maybe solve some technical problems here and there when they arise… the students get 180 days of practice each year" says Moore.

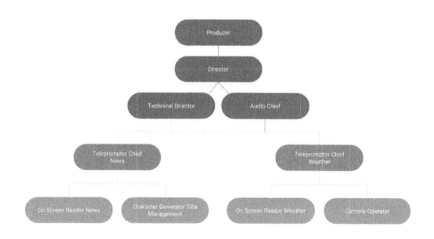

The director's role is the most important role in the organization and it is generally held by a senior in the club who has excelled through the ranks of the broadcast club. If your esports program plan includes live streaming to Twitch, this will be an important role inside the club. This role is held in such high esteem that a wall in the production studio is dedicated to pictures of past directors. The director must arrive at 7:15, which is 15 minutes earlier than the rest of the team. This role is responsible for checking in with every department head to make sure everything is running smoothly and on-time. Here is a list of duties the director is responsible for:

1. Set an example and show initiative
2. Focus
3. Watch the clock
4. Test all systems a safe time ahead
5. Be ready to give warning and cues
6. Delegate
7. Anticipate and solve problems
8. Be able to work all the equipment
9. Learn the terminology
10. Trace cables
11. Watch meters and levels
12. Review past performance and adjust
13. Rehearse and practice
14. Balance praise and discipline
15. Emulate the experts
16. Develop talent
17. Take inventory

As you can imagine, this is quite a lot of responsibility for a junior or senior in high school. However, Moore explained to me, "for the right student, this type of responsibility builds character and prepares them for the real world." Here is a look at a normal day in the Broadcast Club.

- 7:15 - Students begin arriving
- 7:25 - 10 Minute Warning
  - Latest director can arrive
    - Plug in camera
    - Set trims on microphones
    - Adjust credits
- 7:30 - 5 Minute Warning
  - Cameras must be on tripods and visible in the switcher
  - Mic trim is set

- o AV Test; Check cameras, set chroma key, bring up the banner, check ch19, and troubleshoot
  - o Turn off mics on set
- 7:34 - 1 Minute Warning
  - o Switch Leightronix to ch6
  - o Turn off PA speaker
- 7:34:35 - Quiet on set
  - o 30-second warning
  - o Turn mics back on
- 7:34:55 - Countdown from 10
- 7:35:05 - Go Live

Directors in the broadcast club are held to a higher standard than entry-level positions because they have accepted the responsibility of managing others in the club. Team leaders in esports generally assume additional responsibilities to boost team morale and give pre-game pep-talks. The technical director works directly under the main director managing the switching software. The switching software being used at Griswold High School is called vMix.

The next section of this book will be dedicated to the technical implementation of vMix inside the clubs video workflow. This software is also popular in esports and many parallels can be drawn in their implementation. With the oversight of the club's producer and director, the technical director manages the video and audio sources available inside vMix. On a normal day, this would include three camera sources and an audio source coming from the audio mixer.

The technical director and audio chief work in sync, to make sure that the audio sources are set to the appropriate levels. The audio chief sits at the audio mixing board with a pair of headphones to listen to each microphone input and set the microphone trim. The technical director will then mute all microphones onset until the notated time of 7:34:35. The audio chief also has the special responsibility of choosing the music used for the day's broadcast. Teamwork is paramount here and having all club members working in sync is incredibly important. Everyone in the broadcast club needs to have a working knowledge of the entire workflow. Here is a list of items everyone in the Griswold High School Broadcast Club has a working knowledge of:

1. Identify audio and video cables
2. Put together a camera kit
3. Bring up the teleprompter file and hook it into the monitor

4. Cue videotapes / digital recordings
5. Set audio levels
6. Operate the main switcher
7. Ride audio levels
8. Trace video cables
9. Trave audio cables
10. Set up the chroma key
11. Set up lights
12. Update Titles
13. Update public access on both machines
14. Manually focus and adjust the iris on all cameras
15. Recharge batteries
16. Switch Leightronix between Powerpoint, Videonics, and the studio
17. Program Leightronix for public access

During a live interview on the 2018 Streaming Awards show, Moore said, "We started this club originally just as the morning announcements. We started on VHS over 25 years ago. Ryan is the student director. He is a senior about to graduate. Kristin is going to be our director next year." Moore helps train students in the art of video production. In a recent interview, he stressed the importance of developing a "can-do" attitude with the students. Moore has developed what he calls the "3P Pledge" which is posted in the morning announcements classroom. It reads, "We are Professional. We set high standards and emulate the experts. We are Proficient. We are able to use all the equipment in the room and produce high-quality video. We are Proactive. We anticipate shortcomings and problems before they arise and prevent them."

Moore explained to me that there is often a waiting list of students who want to join the club which is why the club makes on-time attendance a high priority. The club has a tardiness policy which is simply, "three strikes and you are out." If students are late more than three times, they will be banished from the club for 45 days. It's that simple. Also posted in the "Morning Announcements Homeroom Notes" you will find this about the tardiness policy: "Office-excused tardies and late buses are all that will be accepted. You are very important in making the announcements flow smoothly. Any arrival beyond 7:30 is considered tardy by me. See me if this presents a problem. All levels - managements and lackeys (future management) - are allowed three tardies. All offenders after that will be ostracized to the general populace for a period of 45 days and remain tardy-free for that time period to return."

Clearly posting rules like this will build trust and responsibility inside the broadcast club. One of the club's members on the Streaming Awards said, "I know personally that being able to be a part of this, coming up from freshman year, has really made quite a difference in my life. Everyone down here that is part of the crew has become like a family. It builds great character. It has helped make coming to school each day even better. This is the place where I found out what I want to do with the rest of my life."

As students rotate through roles and gain positions with more responsibilities the on-air reader, teleprompter chief, and character generator positions, are generally great starting places. The on-air reader role is ideal for students who want to develop their speech and ability to articulate clearly. Students with on-camera positions learn the importance of eye contact. On-air readers learn how to talk to an audience, as opposed to reading to them. Esports programs should consider the value of teaching students how to be part of a team that can live stream or record their tournaments. For students that prefer an off-camera position, the character generator and teleprompter positions are great choices. Operating a teleprompter involves real-time teamwork with the on-air reader.

This entry-level position is a crucial part of the entire workflow and "Broadcast Club Family." Since every Director was once a teleprompter operator or on-air reader, the student-run organization can support itself with the experience required for delegation and troubleshooting. Another student in the 2018 broadcast club class said, "This group helps you build a lot of responsibilities and character because each one of us has our own individual jobs. We are teleprompter chiefs, we have people who are audio chiefs and character generators and I know ever since I became a co-chief that I come in every day and I can do my work a lot faster than I used to be able to do before."

Giving students the opportunity to perform inside a live video production environment is an empowering experience. This opportunity can help students interested in esports the option to naturally branch out into other related interests. Another student said during the 2018 Streaming Awards Show that, "My favorite part is the learning and growing. I remember coming on the first day of freshman year and being told that I was going to be the on-air reader for the day, and I would stutter and it was the most terrifying thing. Then, I came in halfway through my sophomore year as the chief teleprompter, which made it so that if no one else wanted to read, I would have to pick up most of the slack. So that by that time, I learned how to keep learning and growing and making sure that I was literate and able to perform just like everyone else. The experience is important, even if you aren't going directly into the field after you graduate... we can still say that we had this program in high school... so we know how some of this technology works already."

Now let's dig into the nitty-gritty technology that the Griswold High School is using to provide technical jobs for each member of the broadcast club. Many upgrades have been made since the club's first year in 1991, over 25 years ago. Moore still keeps a closet full of analog gear around for the sake of historical perspective. The way the clubs has grown over the past few years is quite incredible. This student-run broadcast club now uses some of the most advanced video production software available in a way that I find ingenious. In the next section, you will see, in more detail, the club's technology set up and how they are able to deliver a morning announcements show to the entire school and local public access television channel station with a production crew of 10+ students.

How the School Uses vMix to Produce Morning Announcements

I have seen a lot of vMix systems in my career and the Griswold High School morning announcements system is one that makes me smile just thinking about it. The school has managed to involve over 10 real-time student-run operational roles. Throughout the production of their morning announcements show, the club is using three vMix licenses, all run on separate computers. The idea of using multiple computers in video production is essential to esports productions as well. Leveraging the power of the school's Local Area Network (LAN), the club is able to connect four computers together into a single video production environment. We will cover networking in the online course, but for now, just understand that each computer is connected together and therefore, able to interact with each other and share resources.

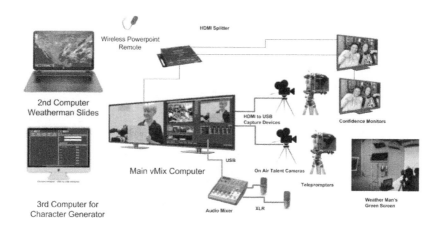

The graphic above illustrates the major parts of the video production system. The main computer is running vMix and is controlled by the technical director using a keyboard and mouse. This computer has all three camera sources and the audio mixer connected to it. The second computer is used to display the weather man's slides for the day. Using a camera with a green screen, the main vMix computer is able to chroma key the weather man's background. A chroma key is a video production process for removing a certain color from a video feed to make that color transparent. The video camera feed for the weatherman can then be layered on top of the PowerPoint slides coming in from computer two. In this way, the school can present the weather just like you see on TV.

The weatherman has a wireless PowerPoint remote control that is used to advance the slides from the dedicated computer running PowerPoint. This computer is running a piece of software called the vMix Desktop Capture app which is able to send the full-screen video directly into the main vMix computer for the technical director to use over the network. You can see the "Confidence" monitors which are in place to show the weatherman what he looks like on camera with his PowerPoint slides behind him. This allows the weatherman to see exactly what he is talking about while remaining focused on his delivery to the camera. If this sounds a bit too technical, or a lot all at once, don't worry. The online training course is going to review this in detail using the same exact software used here.

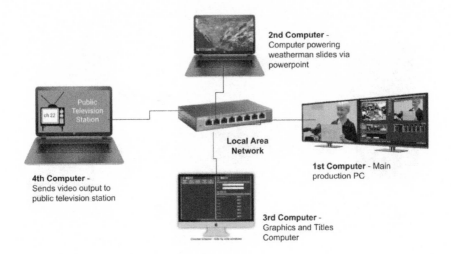

2nd Computer - Computer powering weatherman slides via powerpoint

Local Area Network

1st Computer - Main production PC

4th Computer - Sends video output to public television station

3rd Computer - Graphics and Titles Computer

A third computer is used as a character generator. This computer uses the vMix Web Controller to allow the graphics chief to update titles inside vMix and overlay graphics directly onto the broadcast when they are needed. The vMix Web Controller interface is a compact version of the actual vMix interface, which is accessible to any computer on your LAN (Local Area Network). This means that you can use any computer with a web-browser on your LAN to control vMix.

The vMix web interface has 4 different areas: shortcuts, controller, tally lights, and titles. These can be changed by clicking the icons along the top. For the graphics chief, they are only concerned with titles and shortcuts. The graphics chief can open up two Google Chome web-browsers and split the screen 50/50 to have access to both at the same time. On the title screen, the graphics chief will see all the titles that are currently in the vMix production on the main computer. From here, the operator can quickly edit and change these titles before they are shown on screen.

Chrome browser - side by side windows

http://10.40.4.40:8088/
(shortcuts to activate graphics)

http://10.40.4.40:8088/titles/?key=61c75455-3bec-445f-a954-87bfe3eb0636
(modify lower thirds)

The shortcuts screen will automatically show all shortcuts that have been set up on the main vMix machine. A shortcut is a trigger that can be designed to perform almost any video production task in the software. This allows the club to give the graphics chief access to specific buttons that can trigger almost any action, including fading to the opening video, overlaying graphics, and initiating the closing credits. In the picture above, you can see the shortcut buttons available on the left-hand side of the screen. These include opening, birthdays, lower third, credits, and word of the day.

The word of the day is an interesting portion of the show where the club leverages website data to produce up-to-date information each day. The club uses vMix's "Web Browser" video input to display this information by entering in the address to Dictionary.com's word of the day website (https://www.dictionary.com/wordoftheday). Since this webpage is updated every day, the input will always have a new word displayed in its title each day. So when it comes time to display the word of the day, the graphics chief only needs to click the shortcut button that has been configured to overlay a cropped portion of this webpage onto the screen. The teleprompter chief will check this word and make sure it is included in the script for the on-air talent. The on-air talent will, in turn, make sure they understand the correct pronunciation before the show.

The school birthday title is a ticker that can be updated with information that scrolls across the bottom of the screen. Tickers are used quite commonly in television production to provide additional information in a non-obtrusive way. The graphics chief can quickly update this information inside the title section of their web controller. If there is a birthday that they need to display in this ticker, they can use the shortcut button to trigger the overlay on and off the broadcast, as needed.

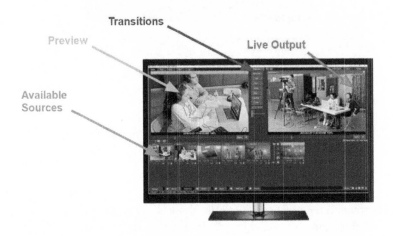

Inside vMix, each camera input looks like a square. Each square has a number that corresponds to its position in the production. When the technical director clicks one of these squares, that input is put into the preview window by default. This preview window is the area that the technical director uses to queue up the next upcoming video input for the production. When the technical director is ready to transition to this video input, they can click one of the transition options, which are conveniently available directly in between the preview and output screens.

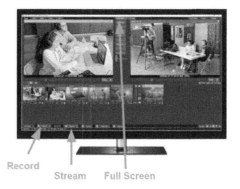

Record   Stream   Full Screen

vMix also features four layers of overlays and 10 layers of multiview flexibility. With the four layers of overlays, the graphics chief has the ability to overlay up to four items on top of the base video layer that the technical director has in the output screen. This is ideal for quickly overlaying lower thirds or ticker titles that may come and go as the technical director switches between the main video sources. Multiview layers work inside each individual input. Using multiview layers, the technical director can have a single input setup with multiple layers attached by default into a new composition. The broadcast club does this nicely with the weather man input. This input is essentially two inputs layered together into one. Using this method, the technical director has just one input to transition to that is built out of the weather man's PowerPoint slides with the chroma keyed video layered on top. Other important buttons that you will learn about in our online course include the record button, stream button, and full-screen button.

The technical director has a total of 15 inputs inside vMix. Five of these inputs are controlled by the graphics chief and the other 10 have been organized into a production workflow for morning announcements. Here are the inputs:

1-4: Camera placeholders (makes shortcuts easier to manage)

5-7: Camera inputs (HDMI internal card, external dual HDMI capture)

8: Opening graphics (Graphics Chief)

9: Virtual camera input with chroma key enabled

10: Credits (Graphics Chief)

11: Birthday Ticker (Graphics Chief)

12: Lower Third (Graphics Chief)

13: NDI in from Weatherman PowerPoint Slides (Weather)

14: Web Browser - (input from dictionary.com cropped for word of the day) (Graphics Chief)

15: Audio Line In

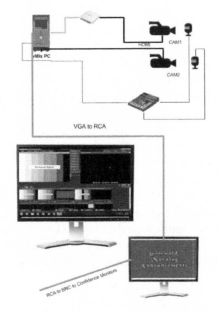

vMix - 15 Inputs

1-4 : Camera placeholders (makes shortcuts easier to manager)
5-7 : Camera inputs (HDMI internal capture card, external dual HDMI Capture)
8 : Opening Graphic (graphics)
9 : Virtual camera input with chromakey enabled
10 : Credits (graphics)
11 : Birthday Ticker (graphics)
12 : Lower Third (graphics)
13 : NDI in from GHS-4003-WX (weather)
14 : Web Browser - www.dictionary.com (cropped to word of the day) (graphics)
15 : Audio Line In - From soundboard (music and mics mixed)

Input 1 set to multi-view using Input 5
Input 2 set to multi-view using Input 6
Input 3 set to multi-view using Input 9 and Input 13
          (This sets up the weather view with chromakey and graphics)

Shortcuts setup:

1: Fade to camera 1
2: Fade to camera 2
3: Fade to camera 3
4: Fade to camera 4 (unused presently)

F1: Fade to opening Graphic (on web controller)
0: Birthday ticker on Overlay3 (on web controller)
F12: Lower 3rd on Overlay1 (on web controller)
F11: Fade to credits (on web controller)
F8: Word of the day on Overlay4 (on web controller)

Secondary Monitor as Confidence monitor
Sent via coax to weather set confidence monitors

It's really quite incredible what can be done with this type of network-connected video production software. This level of video production quality used to cost hundreds of thousands of dollars and therefore, was out of reach of most broadcast clubs. Most traditional video production switchers have a centralized control system. This type of centralized control has traditionally made it difficult to have multiple people working together. Today, school broadcast clubs can build out systems that can integrate teams of students with independent roles working together on a single broadcast simultaneously. This same technology is now being used in esports to connect multiple computers together for broadcasting esports tournaments.

17 HOSTING AN ESPORTS TOURNAMENT

Esports tournaments provide an amazing opportunity for students interested in video games to get out of their at-home gaming area and into a community environment. While many parents see video gaming as a solo activity, there are a variety of ways that kids can now become involved in local community activities. Scott Novism, the owner of Bavous Youth Esports, has started an esports league called Evolve Youth Esports with the noble mission to, "Transform a love for gaming into a true sporting experience." Evolve Youth Esports is one of the many video game leagues that are determined to offer, "more than just video games" to students in their area.

Novism is positive that getting kids together to play video games can help develop social skills. In fact, a recent study published in American Psychologist reports that "70% of gamers play with a friend" and "Playing video games, including violent shooter games, may boost children's learning, health, and social skills" (APA, 2014). Many worry that video gaming, as a sport, lacks the team-based community-building aspects of traditional sports. Parents may still reminisce about how baseball teams would meet up in person at a baseball field each week. This concern is quite valid. The lack of in-person community-based "get-togethers" for many video gamers could lead to what Novism calls "Synthetic Autism." This is a term Novism uses to describe gamers spending too much time in front of screens, which can affect social development skills.

While a common fear among parents is that children who play video games will suffer from social isolation, the studies do prove otherwise. A team of researchers at the Norwegian University of Science and Technology found, "that video games are not the cause of some adolescent issues. Rather, the reason a child spends his or her time playing video games, like social isolation from peers, is more relevant." The study includes data from interviews with 873 students surveyed every two years for six years. The results did provide insights that confirm video games are being used to "fill a child's need to belong and desire to master tasks." The report says "Children who struggle socially are more likely to turn to video games for entertainment" but overall, the study shows video games in a positive light (Science Daily, 2019).

Perhaps using video games as a mechanism to help children meet up in local communities can help build social development skills after all. Many students who play video games at local esports tournaments or gaming centers can build new relationships with friends in their local area. Novism says, "when we bring the students back together… it doesn't take that long… if you get kids in the right environment where they are playing face to face… It is amazing how given the right opportunity, they will teach each other, learn from each other, and grow together…. That is what is missing online… It's the non-verbal teaching that you get from peers that share your interests" (Maricopa, 2019).

When you help your local school or community host an esports tournament or gathering, you could be helping to foster more than just video gameplay. If you look at the experience of bringing children together to learn social skills, student participation and cooperation is more like modern education. Given how attracted children are to video games, competitions and events are becoming a popular way to get kids together in new and innovative ways. This brings us to our next chapter, live streaming your first esports tournament, to make it that much more exciting and powerful.

18 LIVE STREAMING A BASIC ESPORTS TOURNAMENT

If you have never live-streamed video gameplay before, it may seem like a crazy idea. Why would other people want to watch you play video games? It's possible that nobody wants to watch you play video games, but it's also possible that people online are interested in what you are doing. The excitement surrounding live-streaming esports is incredible. For parents and educators, the live streaming aspect of esports opens the opportunity to bring competitive or casual gaming into a new perspective that can connect your program with the world at large. Live streaming an esports tournament also fosters many non-gaming roles for student volunteers such as video producer, camera operator, on-screen talent, announcers, community organizers and much more.

Today's top esports stars have advanced streaming systems that include fancy overlays, interactive extensions, and picture-in-picture overlays. Broadcasters in the esports world can often take gaming to the next level by interacting with their live audience and involving thousands, even millions, of viewers with their gameplay. You can capitalize on the excitement of esports in a group setting when you live stream an esports tournament. This can be a great opportunity to position yourself as someone who understands the esports community aspect of video gaming. Esports tournaments are amazing spaces that can create common ground for generations young and old to collaborate and spend time together.

In this chapter, you will learn how to live stream a very simple production of an esports tournament. Through this process, you can involve students in production, camera operation, social media, announcing, journalism, and much more surrounding the event. You can create a video production team just like a school broadcast club or you can simply manage a one-computer streaming system on your own. Whatever you choose to do, you will find that students are excited by live streaming and the idea of competitive gaming.

Basic Esports Streaming Setup

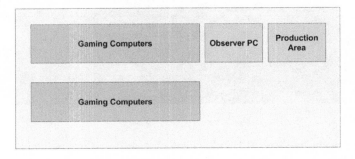

Let's start with the basic concept of adding a live streaming element to an esports tournament. When esports tournaments are in session, there is generally a computer that is dedicated to the task of being an "Observer" of the game. An "Observer PC" is a computer that is connected to the same network as all the computers that are playing competitively. This computer can view the game being played from any player's point of view. During a RocketLeauge tournament, for example, this computer will show sweeping camera views of the players who are closest to the action. This Observer PC can be used by your play-by-play announcer to quickly get an idea of what is going on in the game. The video output of this Observer PC can also be used by your production team to capture and stream the essence of most esports tournaments. During most esports tournaments the Observer PC is connected to a large LCD or projection system for spectators to view.

Basic Esports Streaming Setup

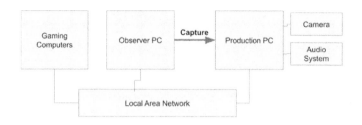

As you can see in the diagram above, the Production PC has a camera and a microphone that is used for capturing a play-by play-announcer (aka the ShoutCaster). While the main screen focus may be the output of the Observer PC, it's very popular to have a picture-in-picture element of the broadcast that includes a play-by-play announcer or an individual player webcam on top of the gameplay. There are a couple of different ways to capture the video from the Observer PC and bring it into your Production PC. In the next chapter, you will learn how to use free software called OBS (Open Broadcaster Software) with a plugin called NDI™. More advanced tournaments will likely use the free NDI Scan Converter software which accomplishes the same thing using less CPU processing power. But for this chapter, the demonstration will use a professional HDMI to USB capture card with an HDMI loop through.

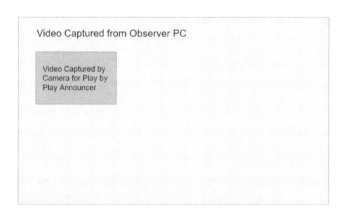

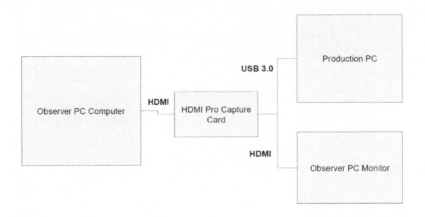

The HDMI Pro Capture Card from Magewell here is used to capture the HDMI going from the Observer PC computer to the Observer PC monitor. The capture card device is able to pass through the HDMI output and produce a USB 3.0 video output that you can connect to your Production PC. Using one of the many popular live streaming production solutions available today, you can mix the Observer PC video with the video from your camera attached to the Production PC.

In your video production software, you should have the following inputs.

1. A camera input for your play-by-play announcer (connected via an SDI to USB 3.0 capture card).
2. A video/audio input from your observer PC (HDMI is used to capture both video and audio) (connected via an HDI to USB capture card).
3. Audio input for the announcer (connected via USB 2.0).

You can use a pair of headphones to mix the audio levels between the play-by-play announcer and the gameplay audio. You can also consider adding some compression on the play-by-play announcer's microphone, but this is something you can learn more about in the included online course.

This is a very high-level look at a simple production for a basic esports tournament. Once your software is set up, you can log in to your CDN (Content Delivery Network) and retrieve your streaming credentials. The streaming credentials given to you by a CDN like Twitch allows you to stream from your video production software securely to your chosen streaming site. This type of streaming is called RTMP. RTMP stands for real-time messaging protocol and it used by CDNs such as YouTube, Facebook, and Twitch for streaming your live production over the public internet. It's important to think about the differences between IP video that is on your LAN (Local Area Network) and video that sent over the WAN (Wide Area Network). The following diagram below helps to illustrate this process.

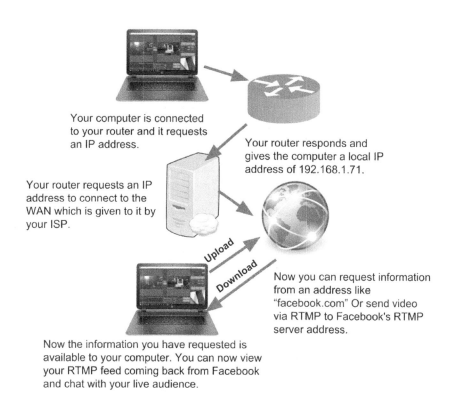

Your computer is connected to your router and it requests an IP address.

Your router responds and gives the computer a local IP address of 192.168.1.71.

Your router requests an IP address to connect to the WAN which is given to it by your ISP.

Now you can request information from an address like "facebook.com" Or send video via RTMP to Facebook's RTMP server address.

Now the information you have requested is available to your computer. You can now view your RTMP feed coming back from Facebook and chat with your live audience.

In the next chapter, you will learn how to capture unique gameplay from each player, add webcam views for each player, and organize a modern esports tournament with your own LAN. At the 2019 StreamGeeks Summit, one of the goals was to provide students with real-world jobs surrounding the esports tournament and that is exactly what you will learn in the next chapter. A troubleshooting guide for live streaming will be included in the online course. If any of these concepts are new to you, I highly suggest taking the included online course.

19 ADVANCED ESPORTS TOURNAMENT LIVE STREAMING

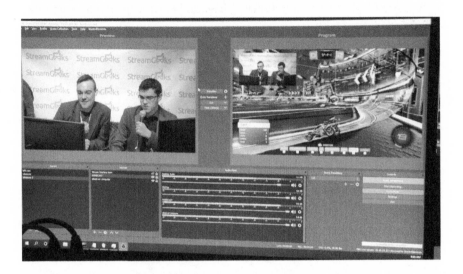

The StreamGeeks Summit happened on November 8th, 2019 in New York City. The tournament featured a 3-on-3 Rocket League setup with seven computers and a production PC all connected on one LAN (Local Area Network). There was a stage area with two student play-by-play announcers on camera holding microphones that were used for audio pickup. The student production crew had multiple PTZOptics NDI cameras available to use in order to zoom into the play-by-play announcers, but also to capture angles that show each of the gaming stations. Students from the S.A.R High School Broadcast Club were able to produce a 100% student-run live stream with the available audio and video sources. The entire student-run production was then live-streamed to Twitch.

So where do you begin?

Let's start with capturing the gameplay of each player and include a webcam video feed as well. With six players spread throughout our venue, the USB capture card method mentioned in the basic setup is not possible. Most live streamers do not recommend the use of more than two USB video capture cards with a single computer. This is due to USB bandwidth constraints with most computers. Instead of using expensive capture cards and video extensions, you can use IP video that leverages the ethernet cabling already connecting every computer.

Each of the esports computers should be connected to a local area network as a prerequisite to hosting the tournament. A local area network or LAN is basically an interconnected system that connects each computer for gameplay with ethernet cabling using networking equipment. This same networking infrastructure can also be used to connect each gaming computer to the Production PC.

In the planning stages of your esports tournament, you will want to know exactly how many computers and devices you will have on your LAN (local area network). Most networks can handle 254 connected devices, all communicating with unique IP addresses, without advanced configurations. The brain behind your LAN is generally a piece of networking equipment called a router. A router is used to manage all of the devices connected to your network. All devices on your network will need unique IP addresses in order to communicate properly. Your router can be used to manage your IP address table and give out IP addresses to devices automatically.

This is not something you generally have to worry about, and it will be covered in more detail in the books included online course. For now, just understand that each device can be assigned an IP address manually or automatically using DHCP. Assuming your router is set up to handle DHCP, it will automatically give any device connected to your network an IP address, unless that device has already been assigned an IP address manually.

Basic Esports LAN Setup

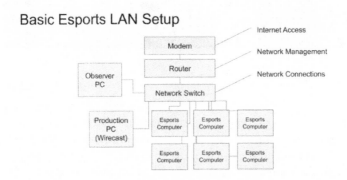

Take the above network for example. The modem providing internet to your router is optional. If you plug a modem with internet access into your router, it will allow you to give all of the devices on your network internet connectivity. This is generally important for esports tournaments, not just for live streaming, but also for updating game software with the latest builds.

Connected to the router is a network switch. Network switches are used to connect devices together using ethernet cabling. As you can see, there are six "Esports Computers" connected to the network switch. Since they are connected to the network, the router will assign each computer an IP address using DHCP. Once each computer is connected to the same local area network, the RocketLeague software will automatically see each computer running the game on the network and allow the students to play the game together during the tournament. Also connected to the network, you can see the Observer and Production PCs. These computers can be used to send and receive video over the network. The Production PC will be receiving video from all seven computers on the network by the end of this setup.

As you can see noted the video production computer is running software called Wirecast. In fact, the students used a streaming solution called the Wirecast Gear for this production. Wirecast is a great software for video production. The students from the S.A.R High School who were operating the system use Wirecast to produce traditional sports productions like basketball during the school year. On each esports computer, you can install a piece of software called NDI Scan Converter to capture the gameplay and any webcam connected to the computer via USB. NDI Scan Converter is a free tool available from NDI that can be downloaded here: https://ndi.tv/tools/.

Once you are running Scan Converter on each of the esports computers, you can choose to customize your NDI video output. NDI can be used as a low-latency video input or output with almost any video production software including Wirecast, OBS, vMix, xSplit, Livestream Studio, MimoLive and NewTek Tricasters. Because all of these computers are connected over the same local area network, our production PC can automatically discover and use all of the NDI video sources on the network.

Another important part of the production connected to your LAN is the Observer PC. The Observer PC can also run Scan Converter to capture the video gameplay and output the video using NDI. The "Observer" feature of the RocketLeague software is available in almost all other competitive video games as well. Observer PCs have become an important tool for play-by-play announcers and esports coaches alike. The Observer PC should be set up to be viewed easily by your play-by-play announcers who will be using the monitor to do their job. Your production team should consider the Observer PC video input as one of the main sources for their production. Just like a regular sports production, you want to give the audience a good overview of the field as the play develops. Transitioning to individual gamer screens should be reserved for special occasions happening during gameplay.

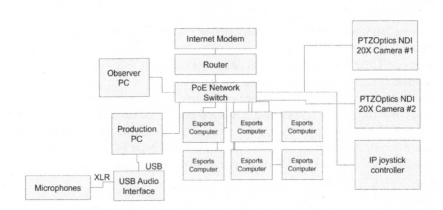

Your play-by-play announcers will have microphones for capturing their performances. Microphones are generally used with XLR connections that can be connected to a USB audio interface. A standard USB audio interface can mix together multiple XLR microphones and connect to your Production PC with a simple USB 2.0 cable. The play-by-play announcers will also be captured via video using a camera connected to your system. In the diagram above, you can see the system has two NDI capable PTZOptics cameras and an audio system for the play-by-play announcer microphones. You can also include microphones to pick up ambiance from the crowd and player's voices during gameplay. NDI cameras can output video directly to your computer without the need for a capture card. PTZOptics NDI cameras also feature PoE (Power over Ethernet) capabilities making them easy to set up with an ethernet cable. This allows teams to connect a single ethernet cable to power the camera, control the pan, tilt, and zoom for the camera and receive video.

Another IP-connected device that gives students an important role in the production is an IP joystick. In this example, there is a PTZOptics IP joystick that is connected to the network. This joystick is able to operate the pan, tilt, and zoom operations of the PTZOptics 20X NDI cameras. Both the joystick and the camera can be powered over ethernet, assuming you are using a power over ethernet capable network switch. The IP joystick uses the PTZOptics camera's static IP addresses to communicate. Unlike the gaming computers that use DHCP to get their IP addresses, devices like PTZ cameras usually keep static IP addresses. You can, of course, control PTZOptics cameras directly inside software like Wirecast or OBS, but a dedicated joystick controller can make your production easier to manage. This way your student producer can focus on the production with a reaction time similar to an esports player. Teamwork makes the dreamwork for esports tournaments. Plus the joystick gives a student volunteer an important real-world career experience as a live camera operator.

Preparing for a Live Stream

The first thing you will want to do before launching your first esports tournament is to create a table for all of your IP connected devices. In the example table below, you can see each device has a name, a friendly name, an IP address, and notes for your team.

Device	Friendly Name	IP Address	Notes:
PTZOptics 20X-SDI	Rear Stage Left	192.168.1.93	Controlled by IP Joystick
PTZOptics 12X-ZCAM	GAMER ZCAM	192.168.1.94	Controlled by IP Wirecast
PTZOptics 12X-SDI	Rear Stage Right	192.168.1.95	Controlled by IP Joystick
IP JOYSTICK	Student Camera Operator	192.168.1.97	Student Camera Operator
NewTek Tricaster	Mainstream PC	192.168.1.200	Main Broadcast Area
Wirecast Gear Production PC	Student Broadcast	192.168.1.202	Esports Area
RocketLeague Observer PC	Shoutcaster	**DHCP**	3 monitors + PC
RocketLeauge PC #1	PC NVIDIA 1	**DHCP**	3 monitors + PC
RocketLeauge PC #2	PC NVIDIA 2	**DHCP**	1 monitor +

			PC
			1 monitor +
RocketLeauge PC #3	PC NVIDIA 3	**DHCP**	PC
			1 monitor +
RocketLeauge PC #4	PC NVIDIA 4	**DHCP**	PC
			1 monitor +
RocketLeauge PC #5	PC NVIDIA 5	**DHCP**	PC
			1 monitor +
RocketLeauge PC #6	PC NVIDIA 6	**DHCP**	PC

Friendly names are incredibly important with NDI devices specifically. Most NDI devices can have friendly names, which will populate in your software automatically notifying you of their purpose.

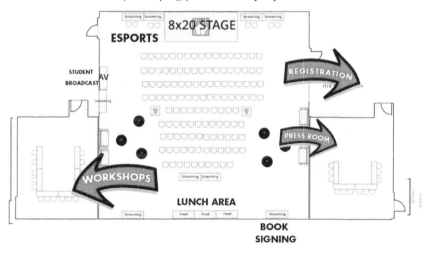

Once you have an IP table ready, it's time to lay out your space and think about cable runs. If you are setting up a live stream in a space that already has esports computers set up, such as a computer lab or gaming center, you may only need to worry about cabling for your live streaming equipment. There are two popular ways to layout space for cable runs. There is software that uses 2D layouts like the picture above and software that uses 3D layouts like the picture below.

I highly recommend learning how to use Google Sketchup if you have time. Google Sketchup Make 2017 is available for free. You can use the 3D warehouse feature to import all kinds of premade objects to populate your space and plan out an amazing event. If you have a student who likes to learn new software, Google Sketchup will provide real-world skills in 3D design and architecture that they can certainly be added to their resume. The course included with this book will include a brief Google Sketchup tutorial, outlining how we built our StreamGeeks Summit layout from scratch.

Once you have laid out your space, you should consider the distance between your networking equipment and the devices you are connecting to your LAN. You may even want to consider putting a row in your IP address table for cable lengths. Once you have your cable lengths determined, it's time to make some cables (or buy them). The course will also include tutorials on how to make your own SDI and Ethernet cables. If you don't feel like making cables, you can always order the cables you need online. Teaching students how to make ethernet cables could be a very valuable lesson for an esports club. It is perhaps the most relevant cable to modern communications and certainly esports.

Once you have assembled all the cables that you need for your event, I highly recommended labeling each end of every cable. This is important for troubleshooting on the fly, as well as for permanent installations where you need to know which cable is going where. If there is an issue with one device, you can always go back to your networking gear and know exactly which cable is plugged into which device.

In fact, while you have your label maker out, go crazy! Label each camera with its NDI-friendly name and IP address. Label every box that equipment will need to be taken out of and eventually be put back in. Label every computer, monitor, power supply, and even the cables designated for each monitor, such as HDMI.

When you start to realize how many cables you will need to connect every computer, camera, and microphone into a complete ecosystem, you may start to feel overwhelmed. Labeling every cable and device helps in a big way. As you build out your checklist, it's much easier to cross off cables on your list that have labels for the device that they go with, to make sure you have everything accounted for.

Setting Everything Up

OK. You have spent hours organizing your devices, labeling your cables, and transporting all your gear to the site of your next esports tournament. You remembered to ask about the location of the internet access at the venue and you are ready to get started. You are planning to run an extra-long ethernet cable to the venue's internet access, but because you are being extra cautious, you are creating a checklist for each section of the tournament.

Before you arrive to set everything up, you should always plan a few meetings. Communication is key when you have multiple people on your team working together. In your meetings, you should be reviewing the layout, the equipment list, and the execution plan. Here is an example of the packing list for the 2019 StreamGeeks Summit:

Esports Section	TriCaster Section	Wirecast Stream	Esports Production Section	Registration Booth Section	WorkShop Section
(X4) PowerStrips	(X2) PowerStrip	(X1) 24-Port Switch #1	(X1) PowerStrip	(X250) Lanyards	(X1) vmix System
(2 each station)	(X3) NDI PTZ Optics	(X1) NETWORK SETUP	(X1) Step and Repeat	(X250) Name Tags	(X1) PowerStrip
(X2) Banners	(X3) Speaker Stands	(X1) WIFI SETUP	(X1) Observer PC	(X2) Pens	(X1) Keyboard Mouse
(X4) Banner Tripods	(X1) 24-Port Switch #2	(X1) 12X NDI Zcam	(X1) Keyboard & mouse	(X2) Markers	(X1) 20X-SDI Camera
(X6) PTZ WebCams	(X1) Tricaster System	(X1) Wirecast Gear	(X2) MICROPHONES	(X1) Guest List	(X1) PoE Switch
(X6) Computers	(X1) Confidence Mon.	(X1) Audio Mixer	(X2) MIC STANDS		(X1) Audio System
(X6) Keyboards	(X1) SDI to HDMI Conv.	(X1) KEYBOARD MOUSE	(X2) XLR CABLES		
(X6) Mices	(X1) Monitor Stand	(X1) NDI ARCADE	(X1) BROADCAST DESK		
(X6) HeadSets	(X1) KEYBOARD MOUSE	(X1) LCD MONITOR			
(X6) Ethernet Cables	(X1) MAGEWELL NDI	(x1) OBS Streaming PC			

CAPTURE					

A packing list like this can be used to organize your equipment by area and assist in organizing your "day of" preparations. Once your packing list is made up, review it with your team so that you are not the only person who knows where everything is supposed to go. Once you have your packing list in place, it's time to create your day-of to-do list. This is a list of everything that needs to be done, at what time, and by whom. Take a look at the following list from the 2019 StreamGeeks Summit.

Time	Activity	Person	Details
4:30 AM	Delivery of equipment from hotel rooms to Gallery	Paul/Melissa	Request Carts from Hotel night before
4:30 AM	Uber Eats Coffee Massive Delivery Order	Michael	
5:00 AM	Stage Build / AV & Lighting	AV Workshop	AV Workshop our vendor to handle
5:00 AM	Running Power (Center Streaming Areas + Esports)	Paul/Melissa/Andy	Run Power Cables and Power Strips to each major streaming area
5:30 AM	Cable Runs & Gaff Tape Down	Melissa, Stuart	Melissa to set up streaming system with help from team
5:30 AM	Workshop Setup	Andy	vMix System, PTZOptics Camera on Tripod, Microphone on Stand, Projector connected
5:30 AM	ESports System Setup	Todd Conley / Helix Esports	Plug in all computer and booth them up. Connect them to network cables
5:30 AM	Speaker Stand Setup / Banner Setup	Sean, Kyle	Speaker Stands are for cameras. Use 1/4-20 screws. Banners are above esports areas and use 3 tripods and center pole
5:30 AM	Broadcast Table Pop Up / 10' Step and Repeat Banner	Matt / Pat	Instructions in bags. This goes next to esports table. Setup table and LCD on it

			with Observer PC.
5:30 AM	Press Area Set up	Julia	Posters and Easels. Sponsors (on Columns). Schedules / Media Space
6:00 AM	Table / Chair Arrangements	All Teams	All teams may need to help arrange tables with tech on them. They need to be in place to go further in our setup plans
6:00 AM	Confidence Monitor setup SDI to HDMI	Matt/Pat	Build cart and connect SDI to HDMI converter. Connect power strip to converter and LCD. Put camera on top
6:00 AM	LED Screen Setup	Be Terrific	One LCD in lobby and one next to esports areas
6:00 AM	Network Configuration	Matt Davis	Should be plug and play. Review IP connections for all computers.
6:00 AM	Poster & Easel Set Up	Tess	Posters and Easels. Sponsors (on Columns). Schedules / Media Space
6:00 AM	MP3 Files on USB Stick (Test Laptop) Play Music on House Speakers	Tess	Play music to get team moving this early in the morning
6:30 AM	Wirecast Streaming System Setup (Camera Focus)	Melissa Paul Richards	Make sure Wirecast machine is connected to all cameras and working.
6:30 AM	OBS Streaming System Testing (Esports Focus)	Todd Conley	
6:30 AM	Audio System Testing (Esports Area)	Melissa	
6:30 AM	TriCaster Steaming System Testing	John Mahoney	
7:00 AM	LiveU Stream Setup #1	Paul	Setup LiveU with Wirecast and make sure it's streaming properly
7:15 AM	LiveU Stream Setup #2	Paul	Setup LiveU with TriCaster and make sure it's streaming

112

			properly
7:00 AM	Registration Area Setup	Sean, Kyle	Set out badges and lanyards
7:00 AM	Streaminng System Testing	Paul / Matt / Andy	Check to see if all NDI sources needed are available properly
7:00 AM	PTZOptics Booth Setup (PTZO Backdrop)	Matt / Pat	Partner Team to layout display and brochures
7:00 AM	Book Signing Area	Tess	Books should be out and ready with a small sign
7:00 AM	Placement of signage (Small Signs for each area)	Julia	Final check over everything.
7:30 AM	Empty Box removal	Julia / Tess	Can we move empty boxes and cartons to the Workshop area or press room?
8:00 AM	General Testing	Everybody	
8:00 AM	Microphone Test	Tess	
8:00 AM	Powerpoint / Projector Test	Sean	
8:00 AM	Start Streaming and Test EasyLive	Tess / Paul	Use Wirecast Computer to log into EasyLive... Check streams and start them
8:30 AM	Paul & Tess Get on stage - Test Microphones	Paul / Tess	**Review announcement speech**
8:45 AM	Paul makes a short speech	Paul	Play short video and presentation #1
9:00 AM	Facebook Panel Starts	Tess	Take speakers onto stage
9:45 AM	Catchbox used for Q&A	Tess	Throw catch box into the crowd
10:00 AM	Business Panel	Paul	Usher next panel onto the stage
11:00 AM	Esports Tournament	Tess	Prepare for Esports Play-by-Play Announcements

Staying organized is the key to successful events. Above, you can see each task starts with the time that the task should be executed. Managing this can be a great experience for students who want to learn the importance of planning and organization. It's important to have someone on your team who is responsible for keeping everyone on pace with the schedule. Students who volunteer can put "Esports Tournament Admin" of "Community Manager" on their resume. This person is usually found with a clipboard, checking off completed tasks and helping along with team members who have questions about the next steps. Real-world experiences like this can help open students' eyes to the possibilities of entrepreneurship and the business of esports. Helping students realize and experience real-world skills is one of the most valuable reasons schools should host esports tournaments.

If you have planned everything out correctly, you should be well on your way to hosting a successful esports tournament live stream.

20 HOW TO DESIGN AN AUDIOVISUAL DIPLAY FOR ESPORTS

Introducing the Esports Spectator Display Rule™

(Photo Credit - Photo by Stem List on Unsplash https://unsplash.com/photos/EVgsAbL51Rk)

Esports can involve an incredible amount of math. Teams are expected to triangulate opponent positions, manage multiple economies, and make decisions regarding a collection of ever-changing numerical values. But bringing mathematics derived from esports into the classroom can be even more challenging in some ways for middle and high school teachers. New esports curriculums from organizations such as NASEF are now available to help deliver tools to teachers in fun and educational ways. In this chapter, you will learn how geometry and physics can be used in a realistic way that could be helpful both in class and in planning an esports area.

When planning out a space for esports tournaments, many overlook the importance of good audiovisual design to accommodate spectators. Unlike traditional sports where coaches and audiences can watch from the sidelines, esports gameplay must use image magnification with large screens for viewers to watch and follow along with the tournament. The challenge for most esports event spaces is to produce a video stream that can simultaneously be viewed on large screens for people sitting in the crowd and small screens for people watching the live stream from their mobile devices. Luckily, esports game developers have recognized the need to provide "observers" with an entertaining spectator experience; in fact, most modern game developers are designing games with the hope that large audiences will be watching online. And even though game designers are thinking about the viewability of online gameplay, they are still primarily designing experiences to be viewed on screens from roughly 12-24" away. As esports becomes more popular, spectators that attend events in person need to be able to view displays that are large enough to represent important details in the gameplay legibly from a distance.

While the actual footprint esports players take up inside an event space may be small, thinking about what spectators will need is important in esports areas of any size. In the largest esports stadiums, crowds generally surround large displays that are above or beside the esports players. Spectators are then able to view the gameplay on these large screens that magnify the video broadcast being produced with live video game screens and camera sources. Most large screens are powered by a video production computer that can output a mix of video cameras, capture devices (gaming computers) and live broadcast graphics. Most game developers offer an "Observer Mode" that can be used to display an intelligent mix of important views of the games being played. In smaller esports areas, a simple projector or large screen LCD connected to a computer running the video game client in "Observer Mode" may be all you need for spectators to watch. Either way, it's important to have a foundational understanding of the audiovisual elements involved with properly displaying an esports tournament for spectators.

Viewing Distance From the Farthest Viewer = 30' (9 m)

To provide the most engaging experience for the audience, spectators should be able to clearly see all the important elements of the game the same way that players can see them in front of their screens. Every game is different, but most video games today use 8-12-point font for detailed inventory items and 12-24 point font for major titles, clocks, and announcements. Font of any size can be hard to read if the viewer is too far away from a screen that is not large enough: as a reference, a 12-24 point font is generally recommended for PowerPoint slides and 10-12 point font is the default size for word processing software such as Microsoft Word. While you can easily live-stream video of esports to other computers and smartphones that people can focus on with screen directly in front of them, people in a room with a projector or television need the size of the display to accommodate the distance they are viewing from. Game developers use small fonts to save space for other visual elements important to competitive gameplay. Spectators of an esports tournament are not viewing screens the same way they would a PowerPoint slide deck.

In the 1980's, the University of Arizona and 3M researchers developed a "24-point font rule" that applied to the 35mm slides that were being produced at the time. The study determined that 35mm slides projected on large screens had an ideal font size that was based upon a minimum arcminute. This minimum arcminute has been studied to provide quick, accurate reading and information absorption for viewers of large screen displays. In more recent times, this study has been used for digital image projections to derive the popular 6:1 (distance to image height rule) that is popular in audiovisual design. Changes to technology, most specifically display resolution, have made these older measurement rules unreliable and misleading. UHD/4K screens have stretched the limits of readability and, as a result, traditional measurement rules like the "24-point font rule" are now generally unusable.

Extron Electronics, a prominent global audiovisual manufacturer, has simplified these studies and pushed aside all of the variables with one simple rule that applies to any digital screen. This new rule states that a *minimum text height of 1" per 15' of viewing distance* (2.5cm per 4.5 meters) is a reliable standard as long as an average arcminute between 10 and 20 (higher being better) is maintained. Extron notes that text which occupies "10 vertical minutes of the viewer's vision" can be legible but "15 to 20 arc-minutes" is a safer rule of thumb. The industry uses "arc-minutes" to measure how legible text on a screen will look to spectators from various distances. The further that you move away from a screen, the narrower your vision arc becomes and therefore the information becomes less legible. Because this rule deals with the final size of text on a screen, resolution and scaling with modern 4K screens are no longer an issue. Therefore, the *Esports Spectator Display Rule* uses the same principles and applies standards that most esports displays can follow as a rule of thumb (Extron, n.d)

Esports Spectator Display Sizing

So how do you appropriately size the spectator display for your esports arena, stadium or classroom? Unfortunately, there is no simple or universal answer. There are many variables that will affect the success of your esports spectator display. These include but are not limited to the following:

- The text size used by the game developers (not in your control)
- The contrast between text and background (not in your control)
- Ceiling height (not in your control)
- The distance to the farthest possible spectator (usually in your control)
- Display resolution (assuming you do not own the display already - in your control)

- Display driver scaling options used on your PC (if available - in your control)
- Available in-game scaling - sometimes called "window size" (if available - in your control)
- Display mounting height (usually in your control)

This may seem like too many factors to manage but with a bit of thoughtful analysis and some research-based information, you can fairly well predict what size of display will accommodate the worst-case viewing distance for an enjoyable spectator esports experience. First, consider what you are trying to control with your selection. Since you cannot control the text size inside the game, the only reliable option is to make sure that the resulting text shown on the spectator display is large enough to read from the cheap seats.

"Well, how big does text really need to be?" might be your next question. How would anyone know that? Luckily, decades ago, a group of university and corporate researchers collaborated to discover how big textual information needed to be when presented to groups for it to be easily ingested, processed, and recalled. While you do not expect to be tested on the current contents of a player's health stats or inventory, you can use these results for any application where readable text is the goal. What researchers discovered is that humans need the height of text to take up a minimum of about 10 arcminutes (or ⅙ of a degree) of our vision to be readable. Bigger than this is even better. Of course, font style and contrast can have a big impact on this as well, but because these factors are baked into the game they cannot typically be modified.

So, with a basic understanding of a single arc-minute being the same as ⅙ of a degree and a prescription to provide at least 10 arc-minutes for the height of each letter, you can break out a calculator and determine the correct esports spectator display size. Unfortunately, there are still too many variables between games to make any universal statement. However, using League of Legends 2020 as a standard baseline of information, by extension the "Esports Spectator Display Rule" attempts to provide a more general prescription for games that use similar font sizing, etc.

League of Legends does indeed provide its own setting for 'Window Size' that scales the game to better 'fill' your screen (albeit sometimes partially and sometimes fully). Using a Windows PC that can scale its displays for easier text reading (in Windows Display Settings), you can see how League of Legends adapts to these settings and what it might look like on today's high-resolution flat panel and projected displays. The table below shows the results:

Display Resolution	Display Scaling	Game Setting	Full Screen	Small Menu ~H%	Maximum Viewing Distance to Display Height Ratio*
1080p	**100%**	**1920x1080**	**100%**	**1.33**	**3.1**
1080p	125%	1280x720	83%	1.04	2.4
1080p	**150%**	**1280x720**	**100%**	**1.33**	**3.1**
1080p	175%	1024x576	93%	1.33	3.1
2160p	100%	2560x1440	67%	0.99	2.3
2160p	125%	2560x1440	83%	1.18	2.7
2160p	**150%**	**2560x1440**	**100%**	**1.38**	**3.2**
2160p	175%	1920x1080	87%	1.18	2.7
2160p	**200%**	**1920x1080**	**100%**	**1.38**	**3.2**

max ratios presented are approximate and are based upon 15 arcminutes of text height of the 'small' menu text in LoL specifically. Other games and other text within the game (if smaller) may not follow this recommendation. Strong contrast between text and its background can have a significant effect on results.

This table displays: the native resolution of the display (e.g. 1080p, 2k or 4k); the display scaling setting used in Windows 10; the game scaling "Window Size" setting used in League of Legends; whether the combination of the two settings result in a full-screen rendering or a 'windowed' game view; a measurement of the approximate percentage of the total display height that one line of text takes up (in this case, the 'small menu' text was measured); and finally a resulting ratio that we can apply to our farthest viewing distance and screen size to achieve our minimum target. This example increased the target from the rock-bottom minimum of 10 arcminutes by a factor of 50% to achieve approximately 15 arcminutes to provide for a more enjoyable experience.

So, what do we do with this ratio? Looking at the bold rows, you can see that all of the "Full Screen" renderings require a 3.1 - 3.2 maximum distance to screen height ratio. Of course, the "windowed" renderings require viewers to be even closer and show the PC's desktop or other applications running in the background, which are undesirable. Let's look at a real-world example... Say that I'm thinking fairly "big" and I hope to have spectators sitting as far back from my desired display mounting location as 30 feet. Using the ratio of 3.2:1, this means that my display must be at least (30' / 3.2 = 9-⅜') or 112.5" in height. For a modern 16x9 display, that also means it will need to be at least (112.5 / 9 * 16) = 200" wide (or in the normal display sizing vernacular 229.5" diagonal).

$$\text{Suggested Display Height} = \left(\frac{\text{Furthest Viewer}}{3.2} \right) \times 12$$

$$\text{Display Width} = \left(\frac{\text{Display Height}}{9} \right) \times 16$$

$$\text{Display Diagonal} = \sqrt{\text{Width}^2 + \text{Height}^2}$$

You may have noticed...this is a very large screen. Over 9' tall and almost 17' wide. Given today's available displays, this means either a flat panel video wall or a projector and screen.

When you begin to install such a large screen, you will discover that you need a very high ceiling to accommodate not just the screen height but the mounting height above the floor as well, so that all viewers can clearly see the screen without obstruction. So, if you have the ceiling height and the budget, you can install a beautiful 220" LED video wall or an ultra-bright projector and screen to accommodate spectators as far back as 30'.

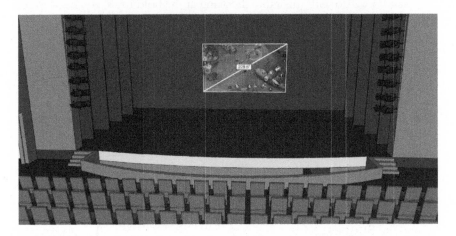

You can also look at this another way by considering that the farthest spectators can sit from a more reasonably sized (and "relatively" more affordably priced) 110" single panel LCD display? A 110" diagonal LCD has about a 54" high image. Using the factor of 3.2, you can sit spectators about 173" (or 14'5") away from the display. At 54" high and a mounting height of 48" to the bottom of the image, you can likely fit this smaller (though still huge) display under a 9' ceiling. Can you sit spectators farther than this 3.2:1 ratio? You certainly can, and no one will be injured by the experience. However, they might find the experience less enjoyable if they are unable to read the on-screen game text.

In conclusion, if you can positively increase proportional scaling from your PC and game combined with a full-screen rendering, and if the text experience in your game of choice is similar to that of League of Legends 2020, then you can use the factor of 3.2:1 (Viewing Distance: Display Height) to achieve readable text for your spectators for an enjoyable eSports experience.

Is your existing spectator display big enough?

Every game is different and many esports facilities already have large screen displays installed, here is a method you can use for testing your displays using the arc-minute rule for viewers in your space: measure the text height and the distance from the farthest viewer and then use a scientific calculator (or the excel sheet included in our online course) to calculate arc-minutes.

$$\text{Arc Minutes} = 60 \times \arctan \left(\frac{\text{Text Height}}{\text{Viewing Distance}} \right)$$

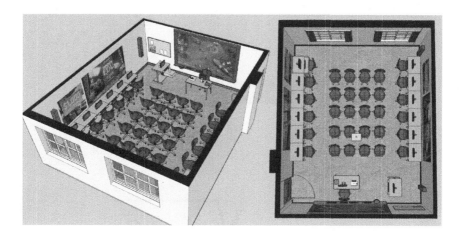

Now let's take an example of a school computer lab and apply the *Esports Spectator Display Rule* in a real-world example. The computer lab is a standard rectangle classroom that measures 20' x 24'. There are 12 gaming stations set up for a five on five League of Legends match with one coach observer computer for each team. The gaming computers are set up on the edges of the classroom with a production computer in the front of the classroom to display an "Observer" view to the spectators. In the center of the classroom, there is a spectator space set up with 20 chairs in five rows of four. The furthest viewer is at the back of the classroom almost 17 feet away from the projector. Because there are so many different types of display resolutions and scaling options, let's assume that you are using a 1080p projector with the default 100% scaling option; therefore, this example can use the ratio of 3.1:1 to calculate our suggested display size.

$$\text{Suggested Display Height} = \frac{17'}{3.2} \times 12$$

Height = 63"

$$\text{Suggested Display Width} = \frac{63"}{9} \times 16$$

Width = 112"

The above equation gives a suggested display height of 63" and a width of 112". With this information you can calculate the diagonal below.

$$\text{Suggested Display Width} = \sqrt{63"^2 + 112"^2} \times 16$$

Diagonal = 128"

This equation recommends a display with a 128" diagonal or 10 foot 6 inches. While again this is a massive display, it just goes to show how large esports spectator displays should be in an ideal environment. In the next segment, you can review tips for accommodating more viewers and optimizing their esports viewing experience.

Other practical advice for esports spectator displays

If you can't fit into a space that is big enough to accommodate the further viewers, consider removing the last row of chairs. Remember that viewers closer to the screen will be able to have a better view and you may want to change your goals to prioritize the majority of spectators. Remember that *contrast is king* when it comes to legibility. While League of Legends, for example, has options that you can use to increase the contrast on the screen, you generally do not have control of the background with which the text can contrast with. Remember that you do not need to affect the competitive video gamer's screens to achieve higher levels of contrast on your Observer PC. In fact, you can optimize the settings on your Observer

PC to increase the size of the HUD display, show a scoreboard, and even team frames. You should also set a frame rate cap on your Observer PC to match the frame rate capabilities available on your display. Higher-end esports productions will use broadcast graphics packages to display important details larger than the game would normally display them for competitive players. Through the process of understanding the video production elements used to live stream an esports tournament, students can gain a better understanding of the role audiovisuals play in their gaming experience.

21 AN OPTIMISTIC VIEW OF ESPORTS AND EDUCATION

Parents and educators have always understood the value of working closely with children and young adults. History has proven repeatedly that massive changes in culture will often be driven by a society's youth. When a generation becomes emboldened by a cultural movement, that they have made their own, there are few powers in the world that can stop its progress. In today's ever-changing online landscape, even more attention must be paid by parents and educators to foster positive student development. With almost 90% of teens today reporting that they have access to a smartphone and 50% admitting that they are "addicted to their devices," there are a too many things that can quickly lead impressionable students astray (McClellan, 2018). Engaging students where they are passionate and preparing them for the interactions, they will inevitably have online is perhaps the best way of shepherding the youth toward a positive future.

The past decade has brought an overwhelming amount of change into the world. Many parents feel this new world of video gaming is alien to their own upbringing and overall understanding of a healthy childhood. Hopefully some of the chapters in this book will help shift this paradigm as parents and educators embrace the future. Hosting an esports tournament is a thrilling opportunity to bridge the gap between students, parents and educators. This type of event could be just what your community needs to "break the ice" and connect generations young and old. Video games are something that everyone can enjoy. Hosting an esports tournament can be done at the grassroots levels, just like hosting a school science fair or a stargazing outing. The parents and educators who can meet students halfway and create common ground will ultimately reach their goals faster and more effectively.

Perhaps sitting down and playing video games with your children isn't as bad of an experience as you thought? There are many opportunities to involve students in experiences that can leverage their own interests in video games for the better. The intersection between esports and education is a place where innovation and excitement flourish. Involving students in career paths that involve technology play naturally into many areas of esports. As educators continue to embrace the esports movement in positive and constructive ways, students will benefit from the learning opportunities provided by this effort. Once educators learn to use this cultural movement to find real world career paths for students inside and outside of the esports industry, the paradigm of esports in education will finally begin to shift in the correct direction.

If you are working on an interesting esports project, consider joining the Facebook group *Esports in EDU* and telling our group about it! Included with this book is an online course all about how you can host an esports tournament in your community in a fun and affordable way. Please feel free to email me directly if you have enjoyed any part of this book. I would truly love to hear from you!

Sincerely,

Paul Richards
Paul.richards@streamgeeks.us

ABOUT THE AUTHOR

Paul is the Chief Streaming Officer for StreamGeeks. StreamGeeks is a group of video production experts dedicated to helping organizations discover the power of live streaming.

Every Monday, Paul and his team produce a live show in their downtown West Chester, Pennsylvania studio location. Having produced live shows as amateurs themselves, the StreamGeeks steadily worked their way to a professional level by learning from experience as they went.

Today, they have an impressive following and a tight-knit online community which they serve through consultations and live shows that continue to inspire, motivate, and inform organizations who refuse to settle for mediocrity. The show explores the ever-evolving broadcast and live streaming market while engaging a dedicated live audience.

As a husband and father raising his children in the Lutheran faith, Richards knows a thing or two about the technology inside the church. Richards now specializes in the live streaming media industry leveraging the technology for lead generation. In his book, "Live Streaming is Smart Marketing", Richards reveals his view on lead generation and social media.

GLOSSARY OF TERMS

4K - A high definition resolution option (3840 x 2160 pixels or 4096 x 2160 pixels)

16:9 [16x9] - Aspect ratio of 9 units of height and 16 units of width. Used to describe standard HDTV, Full HD, non-HD digital television and analog widescreen television.

API [Application Program Interface]- A streaming API is a set of data a social media network uses to transmit on the web in real time. Going live directly from YouTube or Facebook uses their API.

Bandwidth - Bandwidth is measured in bits and the word "bandwidth" is used to describe the maximum data transfer rate.

Bitrate – Bitrates are used to select the data transfer size of your live stream. This is the number of bits per second that can be transmitted along a digital network.

Broadcasting - The distribution of audio or video content to a dispersed audience via any electronic mass communications medium.

Broadcast Frame Rates - Used to describe how many frames per second are captured in broadcasting. Common frame rates in broadcast include **29.97fps and 59.97 fps.**

Capture Card - A device with inputs and outputs that allow a camera to connect to a computer.

Chroma Key - A video effect that allows you to layer images and manipulate color hues [i.e. green screen] to make a subject transparent.

Cloud Based-Streaming - Streaming and video production interaction that occurs within the cloud, therefore accessible beyond a single user's computer device.

Color Matching - The process of managing color and lighting settings on multiple cameras to match their appearance.

Community Strategy - The strategy of building one's brand and product recognition by building meaningful relationships with an audience, partner, and clientele base.

Content Delivery Network [CDN] - A network of servers that deliver web-based content to an end user.

CPU [Central Processing Unit] – This is the main processor inside of your computer, and it is used to run the operating system and your live streaming software.

DB9 Cable - A common cable connection for camera joystick serial control.

DHCP [Dynamic Host Configuration Protocol] Router - A router with a network management protocol that dynamically sets IP addresses, so the server can communicate with its sources.

Encoder - A device or software that converts your video sources into an RTMP stream. The RTMP stream can be delivered to CDNs such as Facebook or YouTube.

Esports – A form of electronic gaming.

Gamer – Someone who plays video games.

GPU – Graphics Processing Unit. This is your graphics card which is used for handling video inside your computer.

H.264 & H.265 - Common formats of video recording, compression, and delivery.

HDMI [High Definition Multimedia Interface] - A cable commonly used for transmitting audio/video.

HEVC [High Efficiency Video Coding] - H.265, is an advanced version of h.264 which promises higher efficiency but lacks the general support of h.264 among most software and hardware solutions available today.

IP [Internet Protocol] Camera/Video - A camera or video source that can send and receive information via a network & internet.

IP Control - The ability to control/connect a camera or device via a network or internet.

ISP – Internet Service Provider. This is the company that you pay monthly for your internet service. They will provide you with your internet connection and router.

Latency - The time it takes between sending a signal and the recipient receiving it.

Live Streaming - The process of sending and receiving audio and or video over the internet.

LAN [Local Area Network] - A network of computers linked together in one location.

Massive Multiplayer Online games – Online games that allows many people to play at once in a shared gaming environment.

Multicast - Multicast is a method of sending data to multiple computers on your LAN without incurring additional bandwidth for each receiver. Multicast is very different from Unicast which is a data transport method that opens a unique stream of data between each sender and receiver. Multicast allows you to broadcast video from a single camera or live streaming computer to multiple destinations inside your church without adding the bandwidth burden on your network.

Multicorder – Also known as an "IsoCorder" is a feature of streaming software that allows the user to record raw footage from camera feed directly to your hard drive. This feature allows you to record multiple video sources at the same time.

NDI® [Network Device Interface] - Software standard developed by NewTek to enable video-compatible products to communicate, deliver, and receive broadcast quality video in high quality, low latency manner that is frame-accurate and suitable for switching in a live production environment.

NDI® Camera - A camera that allows you to send and receive video over your LAN using NDI technology.

NDI®|HX - NDI High Efficiency, optimizes NDI for limited bandwidth environments.

Network - A digital telecommunications network which allows nodes to share resources. In computer networks, computing devices exchange data with each other using connections between nodes.

Network Switch – A network switch is a networking device that connects multiple devices on a computer network using packet switching to receive, process and forward data to the destination device.

NTSC - Video standard used in North America.

OBS – Open Broadcaster Software is one of the industries most popular live streaming software solutions because it is completely free. OBS is available for Mac, PC, and Linux computers.

PAL - Analog video format commonly used outside of North America.

PCIe- Allows for high bandwidth communication between a device and the computer's motherboard. A PCIe card can installed inside a custom-built computer to provide multiple video inputs (such as HDMI or SDI).

PoE - Power over Ethernet.

PTZ - Pan, tilt, zoom.

RS-232 - Serial camera control transmission.

Router – Your internet router is generally provided to you by your internet service provider. This device may include a firewall, WiFi and/or network switch functionality. This device connects your network to the internet.

RTMP [Real Time Messaging Protocol] – Used for live streaming your video over the public internet.

RTSP [Real Time Streaming Protocol] - Network control protocol for streaming from one point to point. Generally, used for transporting video inside your local area network.

Shoutcaster – An announcer for esports games. Similar to a play by play announcer in sports.

vMix® – vMix is a live streaming software built for Windows computers. It is a professional favorite with high-end features such as low latency capture, NDI support, instant replay, multi-view and much more.

Wirecast® – Wirecast is a live streaming software available for both Mac and PCs with advanced features such as five layers of overlays, lower thirds, virtual sets and much more.

xSplit® – xSplit is a live streaming software with a free and/or low monthly fee paid option. This is a great software available on for Windows computers that combines advanced features and simple to use interface.

References

10 Ways Multiplayer Gaming Economies Reflect Real World Economy. (2018, April 9). Retrieved November 11, 2019, from Business

Pundit website: http://www.businesspundit.com/multiplayer-gaming-economies/

2019 World Championship—Liquipedia League of Legends Wiki. (n.d.). Retrieved November 3, 2019, from

https://liquipedia.net/leagueoflegends/World_Championship/2019

A 16-year-old just won $3M playing in the Fortnite World Cup—CNET. (n.d.). Retrieved November 3, 2019, from

https://www.cnet.com/how-to/a-16-year-old-just-won-3m-playing-in-the-fortnite-world-cup/

Aarseth, Espen. (July, 2001). Computer Game Studies, Year One.
    http://gamestudies.org/0101/editorial.html
Baierschmidt, J. R. (n.d.). *Teaching English Through Video Gaming.* 15.

Baker, C., & Baker, C. (2016, May 25). Stewart Brand Recalls First "Spacewar" Video Game Tournament. Retrieved October 31, 2019,

from Rolling Stone website: https://www.rollingstone.com/culture/culture-news/stewart-brand-recalls-first-spacewar-video-game-

tournament-187669/

Breaking Down The Incredible Rise Of Esports | Benzinga. (n.d.). Retrieved October 31, 2019, from

https://www.benzinga.com/general/education/19/01/13008304/breaking-down-the-incredible-rise-of-esports

Call of Duty World League Championship 2019—Call of Duty Esports Wiki. (n.d.). Retrieved November 3, 2019, from https://cod-

esports.gamepedia.com/Call_of_Duty_World_League_Championship_2019

Capcom Pro Tour 2019 Full Schedule and Details Reveal | Capcom Pro Tour. (n.d.). Retrieved November 3, 2019, from

https://capcomprotour.com/capcom-pro-tour-2019-full-schedule-details-reveal/

DreamHack – World of Gamers · Community of Friends. (n.d.). Retrieved November 3, 2019, from DreamHack website:

https://dreamhack.com/

Editors, C. S. M. (2018, November 1). 10 Surprising Ways to Spot a Great Video Game. Retrieved November 11, 2019, from

https://www.commonsensemedia.org/blog/10-surprising-ways-to-spot-a-great-video-game

The Education Arcade. MIT, 2019.
    https://education.mit.edu/
Evo 2020 Championship Series | Official Website of the Evolution 2020 World Championship Series. (n.d.). Retrieved November 3, 2019,

from http://evo.shoryuken.com/

Esports Management: Embracing Esports Education and Research Opportunities. Funk, Daniel. Pizzo Anthony. Baker, Bradley. July,
2017.
    https://www.sciencedirect.com/science/article/abs/pii/S1441352317300670
Extron, Electronics. Video Wall Font Size. No Date. https://www.extron.com/article/videowallfontsize

GameBattles: The World Leader in Online Video Game Competition. (n.d.). Retrieved November 3, 2019, from

https://gamebattles.majorleaguegaming.com/tournaments

Gaming, S. C. 2019-03-11T08:24:33Z. (n.d.). Team SOUL wins the PUBG Mobile India Series 2019. Retrieved November 3, 2019, from

TechRadar website: https://www.techradar.com/in/news/team-s0ul-wins-the-pubg-mobile-india-series-2019

Global eSports viewership by viewer type 2022. (n.d.). Retrieved November 1, 2019, from Statista website:

https://www.statista.com/statistics/490480/global-esports-audience-size-viewer-type/

Global StarCraft II League—Liquipedia—The StarCraft II Encyclopedia. (n.d.). Retrieved November 3, 2019, from

https://liquipedia.net/starcraft2/Global_StarCraft_II_League

Goldman Sachs. 2019. Esports joins the big leagues. Retrieved from https://www.goldmansachs.com/insights/pages/infographics/e-
sports/index.html

HCS Invitational 2019—Halo Esports Wiki. (n.d.). Retrieved November 3, 2019, from https://halo-

esports.gamepedia.com/HCS_Invitational_2019

ESPORTS IN EDUCATION

Hennick, Calvin. Esports Programs Start to Pop Up in K-12 Schools. n.d.
        https://edtechmagazine.com/k12/article/2019/01/esports-programs-start-pop-k-12-schools
High School Esports League Compete for Esports Glory. (n.d.). Retrieved November 3, 2019, from

https://www.highschoolesportsleague.com/

History of eSports. (n.d.). Retrieved October 31, 2019, from http://esportsforgamers.weebly.com/history-of-esports.html

Holstein, M. (2019, June 26). Playing Video Games Is Killing You. Retrieved November 11, 2019, from Medium website:

https://medium.com/tech-critical/playing-video-games-is-killing-you-cb99c6663c2a

Home. (n.d.). Retrieved November 3, 2019, from Electronic Gaming Federation website: http://egfederation.com/

Home—Collegiate Esports Governing Body. (n.d.). Retrieved November 3, 2019, from NAC Esports website: https://nacesports.org/

Hong Kong's libido takes another hit, from herbivores and hermits. (2018, May 27). Retrieved November 11, 2019, from South China

Morning Post website: https://www.scmp.com/lifestyle/families/article/2147743/how-herbivores-hermits-and-stay-home-men-are-

leaving-generation

Is Sitting Worse Than Smoking? – Alternet.org. (n.d.). Retrieved November 11, 2019, from https://www.alternet.org/2013/01/sitting-

worse-smoking/

LCK 2019 Spring—Leaguepedia | League of Legends Esports Wiki. (n.d.). Retrieved November 3, 2019, from

https://lol.gamepedia.com/LCK/2019_Season/Spring_Season

Lee -, P., & Tzialli, rew. (n.d.). The Rise and Rise of eSports | Lexology. Retrieved October 31, 2019, from

https://www.lexology.com/library/detail.aspx?g=110fcda2-6aa3-4652-b071-66760a2479d7

List of esports games. (2019). In *Wikipedia*. Retrieved from

https://en.wikipedia.org/w/index.php?title=List_of_esports_games&oldid=924073533

LoL Pro League—Liquipedia League of Legends Wiki. (n.d.). Retrieved November 3, 2019, from

https://liquipedia.net/leagueoflegends/LoL._Pro_League

Military Video Games Used to Train Troops on the Battlefield. (2017, May 31). Retrieved November 11, 2019, from Defence Blog website:

https://defence-blog.com/news/military-video-games-used-to-train-troops-on-battlefield.html

Must Reads: From video game to day job: How 'SimCity' inspired a generation of city planners—Los Angeles Times. (n.d.). Retrieved

November 11, 2019, from https://www.latimes.com/business/technology/la-fi-tn-simcity-inspired-urban-planners-20190305-story.html

NASEF. 2019. Integrated courses for grades 9-12th.
        https://www.esportsfed.org/resources/curriculum/
Millenials are likely the most studied generation in history. Emmons, Mark. https://dynamicsignal.com/2018/10/09/key-statistics-
millennials-in-the-workplace/
Perrin, Andrew. (Septembre, 2018) 5 facts about Americans and Video Games.
        https://www.pewresearch.org/fact-tank/2018/09/17/5-facts-about-americans-and-video-games/
Playing Video Games Can Boost Fast Thinking. (n.d.). Retrieved November 11, 2019, from

https://psychcentral.com/news/2013/08/22/playing-video-games-can-boost-fast-thinking/58751.html

PlayVS | The Official High School Esports League. (n.d.). Retrieved November 3, 2019, from https://www.playvs.com/

Programs, J. K. C. &. (n.d.). Ultimate Guide to Esports. Retrieved November 2, 2019, from https://info.jkcp.com/ultimate-guide-esports

Ratings Guide. (n.d.). Retrieved November 11, 2019, from ESRB Ratings website: https://www.esrb.org/ratings-guide/

read, R. N. P. A. N. E. L. updated: 8 A. 2018 ~ 1 min. (2017, April 17). Online Gamers May Excel at Teamwork in Jobs. Retrieved

November 11, 2019, from //psychcentral.com/news/2017/04/17/online-gamers-may-excel-at-teamwork-in-jobs/119222.html

r/explainlikeimfive - ELI5: How does internet speed affect online gaming experience. (n.d.). Retrieved November 2, 2019, from Reddit

website: https://www.reddit.com/r/explainlikeimfive/comments/5m1pi5/eli5_how_does_internet_speed_affect_online_gaming/

Schrier, K. (2018, March 22). Playing Video Games Can Make You an Innovative Problem Solver at Work. Retrieved November 11, 2019,

from Inc.com website: https://www.inc.com/karen-schrier/playing-video-games-can-make-you-an-innovative-problem-solver-at-

work.html

Science Daily. April, 2019. Website: Playing video games generally not harmful to boys' social development. Website: https://www.sciencedaily.com/releases/2019/04/190423113956.htm

Selk, A., politics, closeAvi S. G. closeEmily G. analyst at T. W. P. specializing in public opinion about, elections, & policy.EmailEmailBioBioFollowFollow, public. (n.d.). The myth of the lonely gamer playing in solitude is dead. Retrieved November 2, 2019, from Washington Post website: https://www.washingtonpost.com/sports/the-myth-of-the-lonely-gamer-playing-in-solitude-is-dead/2018/03/09/052162e8-1cb0-11e8-ae5a-16e60e4605f3_story.html

Sohn, E. (2014, June 24). What Video Games Can Teach Us. Retrieved November 11, 2019, from Science News for Students website: https://www.sciencenewsforstudents.org/article/what-video-games-can-teach-us

The explosive growth of eSports. (n.d.). Retrieved October 31, 2019, from World Economic Forum website: https://www.weforum.org/agenda/2018/07/the-explosive-growth-of-esports/

The Global Games Market Will Generate $152.1 Billion in 2019 as the U.S. Overtakes China as the Biggest Market | Newzoo. (n.d.). Retrieved October 31, 2019, from https://newzoo.com/insights/articles/the-global-games-market-will-generate-152-1-billion-in-2019-as-the-u-s-overtakes-china-as-the-biggest-market/

The Ins and Outs of CS:GO Tournaments: 2016–2018—DreamTeam Blog. (n.d.). Retrieved November 3, 2019, from https://dreamteam.gg/blog/the-ins-and-outs-of-csgo-tournaments-2016-2018/

The International 2019—Liquipedia Dota 2 Wiki. (n.d.). Retrieved November 3, 2019, from https://liquipedia.net/dota2/The_International/2019

The Overwatch League |—Overwatch World Cup. (n.d.). Retrieved November 3, 2019, from https://overwatchleague.com/en-us/overwatch-world-cup

The Rise of Esports. (2018, December 20). Retrieved October 31, 2019, from NJgames.org website: https://njgames.org/the-rise-of-esports/

The rise of esports as a spectator phenomenon. (2018, December 1). Retrieved October 31, 2019, from VentureBeat website: https://venturebeat.com/2018/11/30/the-rise-of-esports-as-a-spectator-phenomenon/

Types of E-sports games. (2018, July 6). Retrieved November 2, 2019, from Cascade Business News website: http://cascadebusnews.com/types-e-sports-games/

University, © Stanford, Stanford, & California 94305. (2014, May 14). Videogame prepares students to learn about statistics, Stanford study finds. Retrieved November 11, 2019, from Stanford Graduate School of Education website: https://ed.stanford.edu/news/videogames-can-prepare-students-learn-about-statistics-stanford-study-finds

Video game. (2019). In Wikipedia. Retrieved from https://en.wikipedia.org/w/index.php?title=Video_game&oldid=923638998

Video Games Lead to Faster Decisions that are No Less Accurate. (n.d.). Retrieved November 11, 2019, from https%3A%2F%2Frochester.edu%2Fnews%2Fshow.php%3Fid%3D3679

Webber, J. E. (2018, February 5). "Dangerous gaming": Is the WHO right to class excessive video game play as a health disorder? The Guardian. Retrieved from https://www.theguardian.com/games/2018/feb/05/video-gaming-health-disorder-world-health-organisation-addiction

What are fantasy games? - Quora. (n.d.). Retrieved November 11, 2019, from https://www.quora.com/What-are-fantasy-games

What Are The Game Types? (n.d.). Retrieved November 2, 2019, from Discover Esports website: https://discoveresports.com/what-are-the-game-types/

What My Son With ADHD Taught Me About Minecraft and Executive Functioning. (2016, December 22). Retrieved November 11, 2019, from HuffPost website: https://www.huffpost.com/entry/what-my-son-with-adhd-taught-me-about-minecraft-and_b_5846c43be4b0b261c8342778

Winkic, Luke. November 13, 2019. Why Colleges Are Betting Big on Video Games. February 2019.
https://www.theatlantic.com/technology/archive/2019/11/harrisburg-university-esports-players-are-only-athletes/601840/
Stern, Andew.